NEWTON PAGE CLASSICS

THE MISSISSIPPI BUBBLE

A Memoir of John Law

By

Adolphe Thiers

Edited by

Gavin John Adams

NEWTON PAGE CLASSICS
an imprint of Newton Page

NEWTON PAGE CLASSICS
Published by Newton Page

The Mississippi Bubble: A Memoir of John Law
By
Adolphe Thiers

Edited by
Gavin John Adams

Translated by Frank S. Fiske

First published as

*'The Mississippi Bubble: A Memoir of John Law.
To which are Added, Authentic Accounts of
The Darien Expedition, and the South Sea Scheme'*

Published by Newton Page 2011

1 3 5 7 9 10 8 6 4 2

© Newton Page 2011
All revised notes, text, headings, tables and index © Newton Page 2011
All Rights Reserved

Cover image from *Het Groote Tafereel der Dwaasheid,* Netherlands (1720)
'Law, like another Don Quixote, sits on Sancho's ass, being everyone's fool'

ISBN 978-1-934619-05-6
Library of Congress Control Number: 2011922916

Printed in the United States of America
Set in Adobe Garamond Pro

Except in the United States of America, this book is sold subject to the condition that it shall not, by way of trade or otherwise, be lent, resold, hired out, or otherwise circulated without the publisher's prior consent in any form of binding or cover than that in which it is published and without a similar condition including this condition being imposed on the subsequent purchaser.

The scanning, uploading and distribution of this book via the Internet or via any other means without the express permission of the publisher is illegal and punishable by law. Please purchase only authorized electronic editions, and do not participate in or encourage electronic piracy of copyrighted materials. Your support of both the author's and copyright holder's rights is appreciated.

CONTENTS

CHAPTER I   1

Law's birth, parentage and education—His personal appearance and qualities—His early career in London—Duel and its consequences—His travels and financial studies on the Continent—Difference between money and wealth—Banks and banking—Paper money—Law not guilty of the errors attributed to him—His system of a general bank—His attempt and failure to establish a territorial bank in Scotland.

Notes to Chapter I   12

CHAPTER II   17

Law resumes his travels—His success at the gaming-table—Proposes his system to various governments—State of the French finances—Measures of the Regent—Debasing the coin—Its effect—Law offers his plans—Objections raised to it—Establishment of Law's private bank—Its favorable reception by the people—Its benefit to trade—Its extension into the provinces—Astonishing success.

Notes to Chapter II   29

CHAPTER III   33

Law's scheme of a commercial company—The Mississippi Company—Jealousy of, and opposition to, Law—He is sustained by the Regent—The brothers Paris—The *anti-system*—Law initiates a speculation in stocks—Companies of the East and West Indies united—Shares rise rapidly—The Rue Quincampoix—Stockbrokers—Run on the bank—Law triumphs over everything.

Notes to Chapter III   48

CHAPTER IV   51

The national debt—Law's project for redeeming it—Caution necessary in executing the project—The collection of the revenue granted to Law's company—Arrangements for the assumption of the national debt by the company—General eagerness to subscribe for the shares—The nobility pay court to Law—Rage for speculation begins—Stock-jobbing operations of the brokers.

Notes to Chapter IV   61

CHAPTER V   65

Mistake in the details of the execution of Law's project—New privileges granted to the company—Speculation attracts all classes and affects all kinds of business—Foreigners arrive—Tricks of the brokers—Fortunes made in a few hours—Actual value of the shares—Law becomes idolized—Anecdotes—His conversion—Courted by foreign governments—Continued success of the bank—Excessive luxury of speculators—Income of the company.

Notes to Chapter V   77

CHAPTER VI   85

Extravagant prices of goods—First decline of shares—Drain of specie from the bank—Forced measures resorted to—Attempts to revive confidence by adding new functions to the company—*Letter to a Creditor*—Panic increases—Odious measures—Licentiousness of the realizers—Banknotes might and should have been disconnected from the shares—Violent and criminal plan.

Notes to Chapter VI   97

CHAPTER VII   99

The bank and the company united—Price of the shares fixed—Measures for regulating the exchange of shares—Frightful depreciation of banknotes—Debtors the only persons benefited—Father betrayed by his son—Speculators dispersed by soldiers—Second *Letter to a Creditor*—Ingratitude of the *Mississippians*—Murder and robbery by a young nobleman—Firmness of the Regent.

Notes to Chapter VII   109

CHAPTER VIII   111

Circulation of gold prohibited—Reduction of the nominal value of shares and banknotes—Great clamor raised—Whole blame of the reduction falls on Law—Regent yields to the clamor—He retains Law in his favor—Law repeals some of the most obnoxious regulations—Measures to abolish the *System*—Difficulties in carrying them out.

Notes to Chapter VIII   122

CHAPTER IX   127

"Spoils of the *Mississippians*"—Further efforts to bring in the notes—Men suffocated in the crowd at the bank—Mob pursue Law—He seeks protection at the palace of the Regent—Bank closed—Tampering with the currency—Severities towards the *Mississippians*—Final abolition of the System—Law quits France—Confiscation of his property.

Notes to Chapter IX   135

CHAPTER X   145

Recapitulation—Comparison between this and other financial catastrophes—Reflections.

Notes to Chapter X   154

CHAPTER XI   161

Preface to the Darien Expedition and the South Sea Bubble.

CHAPTER XII   165

The Darien Expedition.

Notes to Chapter XII   181

CHAPTER XIII   187

The South Sea Bubble.

Notes to Chapter XIII   237

INDEX   243

CHAPTER I

Law's birth, parentage and education—His personal appearance and qualities—His early career in London—Duel and its consequences—His travels and financial studies on the Continent—Difference between money and wealth—Banks and banking—Paper money—Law not guilty of the errors attributed to him—His system of a general bank—His attempt and failure to establish a territorial bank in Scotland.

CHAPTER I

John Law was born in Edinburgh, in April, 1671. His mother, Jane Campbell, was descended from the famous ducal house of Argyle. His father, William Law, followed the profession of a goldsmith, which, by its privileges, its respectability, and its riches, was equivalent, at that time, to that of the bankers of the present day among commercial nations. William Law acquired a considerable fortune, and bought in Scotland the two estates of Randleston and of Lauriston. He died very young, and left his oldest son, John Law, scarcely fourteen years old.

This son was educated with great care, and manifested a singular aptitude for every kind of study. He hastened to enjoy the independence of his fortune; did not choose to embrace the profession of his father; and preferred to a sedentary and laborious life, one of pleasure, travel, and the study of the liberal sciences. He was handsome, tall, well made, and full of dexterity and grace; he excelled in all bodily exercises, and especially in the tennis court, which was then very much in vogue in Scotland. His mind was not less distinguished than his person; he expressed himself with ease and force, and manifested an extraordinary aptness for arithmetic and the exact sciences.

At twenty years of age he left his mother, and went from Edinburgh to London. He employed his time in gaming, in the society of women, and in studying the mysteries of credit and of commerce. Endowed with an inquisitive spirit and an impetuous temper, he formed an extensive acquaintance, and plunged into great dissipation. Applying a scientific calculation to the plays of the gaming table, he made, without unfairness, considerable sums, but his expenses were still more considerable than his gains, and he ended by contracting large debts. Constrained by necessity, he wished to dispose of the estate of Lauriston, which had been left him by his father. Fortunately for him, Jane Campbell, who watched over him like a tender and prudent mother, came to his aid, paid his debts, and saved him his estate of Lauriston.

The real merits of Law, the charm of his manners, and his fortune, had brought him into intimate association with the principal nobility at London.

A young married lady was the cause of a duel between him and a nobleman, and he was so unfortunate as to kill his adversary by running him through the body. Arraigned before the royal commissioners, he was condemned to death. He was pardoned; but being thrown into prison at the demand of the family of his antagonist, he effected his escape, and fled to the Continent.—(Note 1.)

Law was then twenty-four years old. He travelled through various countries, visited France, still brilliant with the prosperity which sprung from the administration of Colbert, and repaired to Holland to study there the spirit of those proud, rich republicans who had just acquired the inheritance of the Venetians and Portuguese, and covered every sea with their vessels.

Amsterdam was at that time the commercial metropolis of Europe. The interest on money there rarely exceeded two or three percent. She had a bank, celebrated and mysterious, whose credit had withstood the invasion of Louis XIV, whose treasury seemed inexhaustible, and whose system was an enigma even to those who devoted themselves to the study of finance.

Law, in order to investigate more closely the mechanism of this bank, became a clerk of the English Resident, and in this manner added greatly to his knowledge of all subjects connected with commerce and finance.

Law returned to Scotland about the year 1700, being then nearly thirty years old, and having acquired vast information. He was struck with the contrast his own country presented to that which he had just visited. Instead of the extended commerce and the great and active traffic he observed in England and Holland, he found the country poor and paralyzed by inaction.

Scotland, mountainous and almost an island, had a sufficiently productive soil; it was inhabited by an intelligent and laborious population, but needed capital to develop its agriculture and extend its commerce and manufactures. The Scotch, like all mountaineers, were endowed with active faculties, which there was no opportunity to exercise at home, and they expatriated themselves to seek their fortunes in richer countries.

Law attributed the languishing condition of Scotland to the deficiency of capital. He was undoubtedly right; but, confounding capital with currency, which is simply a means of exchange, he imagined that an abundance of money was the cause of the riches of states whose prosperity money had only developed.

He says to himself:

"What is wanting to the proprietor to enable him to clear up his lands; to the manufacturer to multiply his looms; to the merchant to extend his operations? Advances, that is to say money, to pay for the first materials and the manual labor."

"With a few more millions we could pay the laborer who wishes to emigrate, we could retain him upon his native soil, and procure all the material necessary to occupy his labor. Holland, with a sterile soil, whose low banks expose it constantly to the dangers of the flood, is the richest country in the world. Why? Because she overflows with money."

"By what means can money be supplied? It is credit; it is the establishment of banks which give to paper the value and efficiency of specie."

Law thus involved himself by degrees in an error which the appearance of an abundant currency often occasions. He thought that the prosperity of a country depended upon the amount of money in circulation, and that this amount might be increased at pleasure. However, money is not food which will nourish a man, cloth which will clothe him, tools with which he can work; money is the equivalent which, by way of exchange, serves to procure all these things; but the things themselves must first exist. Cover a desert isle with all the gold of the Americas, or with all the notes of the Bank of England, and we should not at once find roads, canals, husbandry, manufactures—in a word, business. If by any means the amount of money in a country could be increased without a proportionate increase in the amount of everything else, the prices would only be raised without increasing actual wealth, because a greater quantity of cash would be put in the balance with the same quantity of merchantable articles.

Money, then, is not wealth; it is the result of wealth, and increases gradually with wealth. In proportion as business activity increases and industry and commerce become more developed, the products, more numerous, must be exchanged more frequently and with greater rapidity; traffic must increase in the same proportion as production. Then money, the medium of exchange, must become more abundant, because it is always attracted where it is needed. Soon, to money, a slow and expensive means of exchange, must succeed bills, means easy, prompt, and above all, economical. Banks will certainly be established: they are the result of an anterior prosperity, and serve effectively to increase it, but never precede it, because the creation of products must precede the demand for their circulation.

If Law, deceived by the first appearances of an expanded currency, attributed too great results to money alone, he was not mistaken as to the means of increasing it by credit. He had explained and developed, in a remarkable pamphlet, the operation of banks better than it had ever been done before.

There are, as every one knows, *banks of deposit and banks of discount.* One deposits his cash in the first, and takes a certificate of deposit, which serves the purposes of cash in making payments. The advantage of these banks is, that they substitute for coin, paper which represents its value, and is at the same time more easily transported and counted. The utility of banks of discount is entirely different. A bank of this kind examines commercial bills, that is, promises to pay, subscribed by one person in favor of another, and if it considers them good, it gives for them, in consideration of interest, the value in notes which bear its own guaranty and are current as money. This is what is called discount. Its function is to change commercial bills and notes, which are not current as money, into its own notes, which are current, and thus enable them to be changed for anything else. In order to do this with security, it must have funds which are responsible for mistakes which it is liable to make in accepting worthless paper. Beside, as the notes it issues depend upon the public confidence for their circulation, it must always be ready to convert them into coin at the wish of the holder, and it is for this purpose that it holds its specie reserve. Its funds should always meet the losses it may sustain, and its specie reserve should always suffice for the redemption of notes which the holders are disposed to present for specie.

When confidence is established, holders of notes do not wish to exchange them for specie, except when they desire smaller sums, or for some purpose where specie alone can be used.

Thus, the specie reserve need be only sufficient for the requirements of traffic, in paying sums smaller than the notes, or for meeting certain special necessities. A bank of discount, then, effects an actual increase of currency, or, in other words, increases the facilities of exchange by metamorphosing commercial bills into bank notes circulating as readily as coin itself.

One advantage of the establishment of banks, Law appreciated as much as the increase of currency—that was the introduction of paper money. Law esteemed this of special importance. Paper, in fact, can be transported to any distance without difficulty; it is easily counted; it is not merchandise, like the precious metals, whose value changes according to the quantity in the market. For all these reasons Law thought it preferable to gold and silver for the requirements of business.

He was right in many respects, and, notwithstanding his high estimation of the virtues of paper money, he did not fall into an error his commentators and enemies have attributed to him.

This error, less common now than formerly, consisted in the belief that, as the fixed value of specie is ideal, and is useful only to be exchanged for supplying our wants, paper money also, which was equally current and could be exchanged for bread, meat and clothing, had an intrinsic value as positive as that of gold or silver. But Law understood perfectly well that specie had an intrinsic value which paper money could not have; that coin melted down is still valuable as an ingot, while paper is worthless when it ceases to be a note, and that this intrinsic value of the precious metals makes them the most certain and secure medium of exchange. He has explained precisely his opinion, on this subject, in a pamphlet still in existence; but he thought that banks could impart a real value to paper. In effect, the notes a bank discounts are assignments of an anticipated product; a bank, in accepting them and issuing its own notes in their place, guaranties the products. If it miscalculates, its capital is responsible. It is an insurance fund against its mistakes. Paper money thus acquires, by means of banks, the actual value of gold. It was upon these conditions, and these alone, that Law thought paper money preferable to specie.

By comparing the results of his observations in the different countries of Europe, his views were remarkably expanded, and he had conceived the vastest system of credit that had ever been imagined. He had observed that the capitals of some great countries had banks, as at London and Amsterdam, but that the provinces in England and Holland did not participate in the advantages of this system of credit.

He thought that by establishing a general bank, which should have its branches in second-rate cities, the advantages of paper money would be extended throughout an empire, even to the small towns and villages.

If a bank at the capital, with a hundred million francs in specie, could issue two hundred millions in bills, the general bank which he had planned could, he thought, in a country which had a thousand million francs in coin, issue two thousand millions in bills, and thus triple the facilities of exchange. In this way, the bills being sufficient for the principal circulation, all the coin of the country would be a specie reserve, except what was necessary for small change. This project was well planned and very practicable. Only Law exaggerated the possible extent of the use of paper money, and had too much confidence in the ease with which it might be put in circulation in remote districts.

Law would have a bank of such importance, a public

institution, and the provincial treasuries for its corresponding branches. These principles stated, he deduced from them immense consequences. In the first place, most governments leased the collection of their revenue to companies of men called farmers of the revenue, who reaped therefrom considerable profits, and inflicted outrageous vexations upon the taxpayers.

The collection of the revenue could be confided to the general bank, and the profits therefrom saved to the state. The payment of the public expenses could also be made by the bank, through its correspondence with its branches. It would thus have the management of all the public money. The farmers of the revenue, to whom was leased the impost duty, exacted a usurious interest of the state when it needed any advances. The new bank would discount the impost as it discounted bills of exchange; it would be possible for it to do this at a still more moderate charge, as in augmenting the amount of specie it would itself have contributed to reduce the interest on money. It could also be entrusted with the care of the loans, and, in this particular, avoid the extortions of the usurers. This is not all; the system of monopolies being generally practised in Europe, and the greater part of the commerce with remote parts of the world being carried on by chartered companies, to whom government gave, on certain conditions, exclusive privileges, this same general bank could have the privileges of special lucrative commerce, and join to its numerous attributes that of trade. Combining thus the profits of a bank of discount with those of the administration of the public revenue and those of its commerce as a privileged company, it would necessarily have an immense capital, which it would distribute in shares among which would be divided its profits. In this manner it would offer its notes to those who desired a circulating medium, and its shares to those who sought a profitable investment.

Such is the ingenious and efficient system conceived by

Law, which united and placed on the same basis both public and private credit; which reduced the different methods of making payments, which, before then, were slow, laborious and complicated, into one only; which furnished coin for the payment of small sums, and banknotes for that of large; which multiplied capital by simplifying the currency; which reduced thenceforth the interest on money, and added to the introduction of an abundant and convenient currency the creation of a means of investment at once sure and profitable.

Even at the present day we except from this system only the leasing of the collection of the public revenues, which is no longer permitted, and the monopolies, which were required at that time, as companies with extraordinary powers were necessary to penetrate unexplored and unfrequented parts of the world.

Full of these views, Law presented a plan adapted to the wants of his own country about the year 1700. This plan was to constitute a company with power to collect the public revenue, to carry on certain kinds of commerce with exclusive privileges, to direct manufactures, certain commercial enterprises, the fisheries, etc. His plan, although rejected, attracted public attention to him, and brought him in contact with the principal persons in Scotland.

In 1705 it was proposed to establish a territorial bank. Law offered a well-digested plan for one, in a very curious pamphlet entitled, *Considerations Upon Hard Money*. Aside from the error which we have mentioned, and which was disposed to attribute the prosperity of states exclusively to the abundance of money, the means of increasing this abundance by banks are clearly explained, and with an understanding of the subject very uncommon at that time. This new plan of Law was no better received than the first. It was rejected, from the apprehension, it was said, of giving too much power to the court.—(Note 2.)

NOTES TO CHAPTER I

(1.) Law's Duel and its Consequences: A Mrs. Lawrence was the occasion of a quarrel between him and Mr. Edward Wilson, fifth son of Thomas Wilson of Keythorpe, in the County of Leicester, which led to a hostile meeting betwixt the parties in Bloomsbury Square, 9th April, 1694, when Mr. Wilson was killed on the spot.

Mr. Law was immediately apprehended, and was brought to trial before the King and Queen's Commissioners, who sat at the Justice Hall in the Old Bailey, on the 18th, 19th and 20th of April, 1694. In the proceedings published by authority, the statement is thus given: John Law, of St. Giles's-in-the Fields, gentleman, was arraigned upon an indictment for murder, for killing Edward Wilson, gentleman, commonly called Beau Wilson, a person who, by the common report of fame, kept a coach and six horses, maintained his family in great splendor and grandeur, being full of money—no one complaining of his being their debtor, yet from whence he had the effects which caused him to appear in so great an equipage is hard to be determined. The matter-of-fact was this: some difference happened to arise between Mr. Law and the deceased concerning a Mrs. Lawrence, who was acquainted with Mr. Law; upon which, on the 9th of April instant, they met in Bloomsbury Square, and there fought a duel, in which Mr. Wilson was killed. It was made appear also that they had met several times before, but had not opportunity to fight; beside, there were several letters sent by Mr. Law, or given to Mr. Wilson by him, which letters were full of invectives and cautions to Mr. Wilson to beware, for there was a design of evil against him; and there were two letters sent by Mr. Wilson, one to Mr. Law, and the other to Mrs. Lawrence. Mr. Wilson's man, Smith, swore that Mr. Law came to his master's house, a little before the fatal meeting, and drank a pint of sack in the parlor; after which, he heard his master say, that he was much surprised with something that Mr. Law had told him. Captain Wightman, a person of good information, gave an account of the whole matter. He said that he was a familiar friend of Mr. Wilson—was with him and Mr. Law at the Fountain Tavern in the Strand, and after they had stayed a little while there Mr. Law went away. After this, Mr. Wilson and Captain Wightman took coach and were driven toward Bloomsbury, where Mr. Wilson stepped out of the coach into the square, where Mr. Law met him; and before they came together, Mr. Wilson drew his sword and stood upon his guard. Upon which Mr. Law immediately drew his sword and they both passed together, making but one pass, by which Mr. Wilson received a mortal wound in the upper part of the stomach, of the depth of two inches, of which he instantly died. The letters read in court were full of aggravations on both parts, without any name subscribed to them. There were other witnesses that saw the duel fought, who all agreed in their depositions that they drew their swords, and passed at each other, and presently Mr. Wilson was killed. This was the sum of the evidence for the crown.

Mr. Law, in his defence, declared that Mr. Wilson and he had been together several times before the duel was fought, and no quarrel ever took place between them till they met at the Fountain Tavern, which was occasioned about the letters; and that his meeting with Mr. Wilson in Bloomsbury was merely an accidental thing, Mr. Wilson drawing his sword upon him first, by which he was forced to stand in his own defence—that the misfortune did arise only from a sudden heat of passion, and not from any malice prepense. The court acquainted the jury, that if they found Mr. Law and Mr. Wilson did make an agreement to fight, though Mr. Wilson drew first, that Mr. Law killed him, he was by the construction of the law guilty of murder; for if two men suddenly quarrel, and one kill the other, this would be but manslaughter: but this case seems to be otherwise, for there was a continual quarrel carried on betwixt them for some time before; therefore, must be accounted a malicious quarrel, and a design of murder in the person that killed the other.

The trial lasted long and the prisoner had persons of good quality who gave a fair account of his life in general, and that he was not given to quarrelling, nor a person of ill behavior. The jury having considered of a verdict very seriously, found that Mr. Law was guilty of murder, and sentence of death was passed on him, 20th April, 1694.—Wood.

In the *London Gazette* on Monday, the 7th of January, 1695, a reward of fifty pounds was offered for the apprehension of Capt. John Law, a Scotchman, lately a prisoner in the King's Bench, for murder; who is described as "a very tall, black, lean man, well shaped, above six foot high, large pock-holes in his face, big, high nosed, speaks broad and loud." This description, which conveys no very favorable idea of Law's personal appearance, and differs from his real portrait, is supposed by Mr. Wood to have been drawn up with a view to facilitate his escape. The prefix of captain, which is otherwise a good travelling title, may also perhaps be explained on the same hypothesis.—*Encyclopedia Britannica.*

(2.) Law's Territorial Bank: Law's proposal for a territorial bank was, that commissioners, to be appointed by an act, under the control of parliament, should be empowered to issue notes, either in the way of loan, at ordinary interest, or upon landed security; the debt not, however, to exceed half, or at most, two-thirds of the value of the land, or upon land pledges, redeemable within a certain period, to the full value of the land; or lastly upon the sale irredeemably to the amount of the price agreed upon. Paper money thus issued and secured would, he conceived, be equal in value to gold and silver money of the same denomination, and might even be preferred to these metals as not being like them liable to fall in value.—*Encyclopedia Britannica*.

CHAPTER II

Law resumes his travels—His success at the gaming-table—Proposes his system to various governments—State of the French finances—Measures of the Regent—Debasing the coin—Its effect—Law offers his plans—Objections raised to it—Establishment of Law's private bank—Its favorable reception by the people—Its benefit to trade—Its extension into the provinces—Astonishing success.

CHAPTER II

Thereupon, Law left home and recommenced his travels, either to gain more knowledge or to present his system acceptably to some of the principal states on the Continent, ruined by the wars of Louis XIV, and very ignorant in all matters connected with credit. He went to Brussels, and from Brussels to Paris. He gave himself up to gaming at the latter capital, and, thanks to his genius for calculation, he won large sums. He held the faro bank at the house of Duclos, a celebrated courtesan of that period, and never commenced playing without a hundred thousand francs.

He even had made some gold counters, worth eighteen louis, for greater convenience in counting. He established relations with several gentlemen of the court, and, above all, with the Duke of Orleans, who liked inventive minds, and was disposed to adopt his views. It was at the time of the war of the succession. Chamillart, overcome by the burden of the finances, was ready to resign the charge of them. Law offered his plans, but no one was in a condition to comprehend them; besides, he was a Protestant, and Louis XIV would not listen to him. Soon, even, suspicions were excited concerning the stranger, who displayed the greatest luxury, and won large sums from the courtiers; and the intendant of the police, M. d'Argenson, sent an order to Law requiring him to leave Paris within twenty-four hours. Law repaired to Italy, and continued to game, whether at Genoa or at Venice, and won immense sums. He then went to Turin, where he lent money to the famous Vendôme, and succeeded in having himself presented to Victor Amédée, to whom he proposed his system of finance. Amédée replied that the system was not adapted to a country in the midst of the Alps, and dismissed him, advising him to take his plans to France or Germany.

The Emperor was then occupied in establishing a bank. Law hastened to submit his views to him: succeeded no better than with the other princes to whom he had presented them, and again returned to his own country. It was said that the sums which he had won at the gaming table amounted to two millions. He transferred these two millions to France, and prepared to return there himself. The death of Louis XIV, the accession to power of the Duke of Orleans, and the deplorable state of the French finances, made him hope that, at last, he should find a country disposed to adopt his measures.

The old king had just expired, in 1715. The war of the succession was ended. During this ruinous war, Demarest, who had succeeded Chamillart, had had recourse to all expedients for raising money. He had frequently renewed the forms of the mortgages on the treasury, in order to revive the confidence of the usurers. He had issued government stocks under every name and form, in order to give them a little credit; but these expedients were exhausted, and the royal stocks were at a discount of from 70 to 80 percent. Demarest presented, on the 20th of September, a desperate report for the year, of which the following is the substance: expenses, 148 millions; receipts anticipated, except 3 millions; 710 millions of royal stocks payable during the current year; whole districts depopulated, commerce ruined, troops unpaid and ready to revolt. In this extremity, bankruptcy was proposed to the regent. It was urged that a sovereign is not surety for the blunders of his predecessors, and that a severe example would render capitalists less ready to lend themselves to the caprices of a spendthrift ruler. The courtiers, who hoped that the relief of the treasury would permit a renewal of favors to them, insisted upon bankruptcy. The regent spurned so unworthy an expedient, and held himself bound by the engagements of the late king. He also refused to give a forced credit to stocks already due, for that would create a paper money discredited in advance.—(Note 1.)

He first set himself about paying the troops, and the arrearages due on some annuities. In order to procure the means, he ordered the revenue of the year to be paid into the treasury although previously mortgaged. This was certainly a partial bankruptcy, but it was inevitable. He ordered the reduction of many annuities, and of almost all those which were at an exorbitant interest; he ordered that the stocks already due should be revised and reduced, and then be converted into 250 millions of notes, in one form called national notes, successively redeemable and bearing an interest of four percent; he established a court for the purpose of prosecuting and fining the brokers who had made disreputable fortunes by their traffic in these securities. At that time, governments used to take such high-handed measures; pressed by imperative necessity, they would yield to the hard conditions which the usurers imposed upon them; but, the time of distress once passed, they took back, by force, that which the usurer had wrung from them by extortion.

We see that the regent, without consenting to a general and absolute bankruptcy, had recourse to partial non-payments, depending upon the importance and character of the debts.

As it was impossible to fulfill all the obligations contracted in the last reign, he endeavored to make the necessary distinctions between them as just as possible; and reducing some and postponing others, he failed to meet only the engagements which were impracticable. Among the measures which he adopted, there was one, however, as dishonest as it was impolitic: this was changing the value of the coin. The practice of resorting to this measure, which prevailed at that period, is the only excuse for the regent.

Governments, for several centuries, forgetting that the value of bullion did not depend upon their decrees, but upon commerce, recoined money, raised it to a fictitious nominal value, and poured it into circulation at a price very much greater than its actual value. But these expedients served only to create a financial derangement, without any real advantage to the government.

The overvalued denomination of coins added nothing to their real worth; the price of everything rose in proportion, and the same amount of gold and silver was always necessary to purchase the same articles. No one suffered by the wrong except such creditors as were compelled by previous contracts to receive specie at its nominal value. The government realized scarcely any benefit from the fraud, because counterfeiters recoined money themselves, and thus made the profit which the reduction in the weight of coin offered them. This crime, called uttering debased coin, was punished by the severest penalties, in vain. The regent commanded that the thousand millions then in circulation in France should be converted into twelve hundred millions. The government ought thus to have realized a profit of two hundred millions, as it issued twelve for every ten required. But only a small part of the thousand millions found its way to the mint; the Dutch and the counterfeiters made most of the illegitimate profit.

But, notwithstanding these measures, the difficulties were only postponed. The annual interest on the debt, reduced and readjusted, still amounted to eighty millions—that is to say, to about one-half the revenue. The royal stocks, converted into two hundred and fifty millions of national scrip, continued to be at a discount of from seventy to eighty percent. Public and private credit were annihilated.

The regent, who wished to test the presbysynodic system of the Abbé St. Pierre, and divide the administration of government among several councils, had placed the Duke of Noailles at the head of the Council of Finance. The Duke proposed some very wise but very slow plans of economy. The exigencies of the situation demanded means for a more speedy extrication from the immediate difficulties. It was at this moment that Law presented his system. Law by no means despaired of France, the most fertile and most thickly populated country in Europe, as well as the most industrious. Although in a desperate situation for the moment, this beautiful kingdom still had three times the revenue of England. In order to revive industry, and relieve the oppressions under which it was ready to succumb, it was only necessary, according to Law, to reestablish confidence and a sound currency by means of a good system of credit.

The genius and enterprising spirit of the people rendered them peculiarly fit to adopt a new and grand theory. Repulsed by the late king, Law flattered himself that he should be well received by the regent. The Duke of Orleans was gifted with a keen, bold spirit; a foe to the prejudices from which he had suffered oppression in his youth, he had devoted himself to the study of the natural sciences, of chemistry and of alchemy, to such an extent even as to be accused of complicity with poisoners. He had studied, above all, the principles of government. He knew Law, appreciated his genius, was pleased with his person, and admired his theories. A system, the principles of which were sound in part, and which could do no harm except by a misapplication of those principles, was certain to catch the adventurous spirit of the Prince, and it had completely seduced him. The increasing independence of thought, the taste for novelty, the license of manners, results of a too sudden emancipation from a too rigid constraint, signally favored the experiment which was to change for a moment, the face of France.

Law did not propose any half-way measures. He offered his project entire; that is to say, a bank which should discount, should collect the national revenues, should carry on commercial monopolies, and afford, at the same time, a plentiful circulation of paper money and a means of profitable investment. The council of finance, composed of sagacious but timid men, did not comprehend the project of Law, or were frightened by it, and decided to reject it. Law then reduced the extent of his plans. He proposed simply a bank of discount, and even offered to establish it at his own expense. He presented several memorials on the subject, which contain little to instruct us today, yet they are models of reasoning. He maintained that a bank would increase the currency by the issue of its notes, would render the remittances from one province to another more convenient, would reestablish confidence by the creation of money of a fixed value—*bank money*; would permit foreigners to make their contracts in France with a basis of fixed and certain value, and would contribute by all these means to the restoration of public and private credit. Law wished to make this experiment at his own risk and peril, and offered his property as a guaranty against any loss which might result.

A member of the parliament of Paris, discussing Law's project, raised some objections to it, which it is interesting to recall, as illustrating the history of the stagnating influence of routine. Among other inconveniences, he insisted that a bank could not redeem its notes if everybody should wish to realize them at the same time; its treasury would tempt the rapacity of government; and, last of all, that its bills would incur a danger which attaches to paper, viz. that of being more easily lost, stolen, or burned than specie. This shows what sort of financiers Law had to do with. He answered these objections, and succeeded in convincing the regent. His plan of a bank of discount was adopted, and he was authorized to establish one at his own expense. The charter was issued by an edict of the 2nd of May, 1716. The capital was fixed at six millions of francs, and was divided into twelve hundred shares of five thousand francs each. He was authorized to discount bills of exchange, to keep accounts with merchants, by means of what was then called a "bank clearing," and to issue notes payable to bearer in coin (so said the edict) of the *weight and denomination of that day*. Thanks to this last clause, the variations in the value of money were no more to be feared by those who should stipulate for bank money, since they were certain, thus to contract according to the rates of coin on the 2nd day of May, 1716. Beside, this guaranty offered to foreigners, there was another assured them; the notes of the bank and the amounts on deposit were exempted from the right of confiscation. The offices were of, and in, the house of Law. The Duke of Orleans accepted the title of patron of the new institution.—(Notes 2 and 3.)

Everything at this time made the necessity of a bank of discount apparent, whether it was the high rates for money, or the uncertainty in the value of coin. Thus the establishment of Law could not fail to succeed. The government was the first to make use of the notes; it received and disbursed them. The holders of the bills, having found the greatest facility in realizing them at the bank, acquired confidence and diffused it. People began to be proud of this paper, so readily converted into specie, and were glad to make use of it, on account of the promptness of payments which it introduced. It had, moreover, an advantage very much felt: that was, its redemption in coin of a fixed value. The constant variation in the price of coin rendered it uncertain upon what basis a contract was made. By stipulating for bank notes, it was certain that the contract was payable in coin of the weight and denomination of the 2nd of May, 1716.—(Note 4.) This was a powerful reason for everybody to contract with that stipulation, and even to deposit their specie at the bank to obtain the notes. Foreigners, who had not dared to trade any more with Paris, on account of the uncertainty of values, also contracted for bank notes, and resumed the current of their business with France.

The circulation thus, by degrees, became established. The moderate charge for discount also had a most beneficial influence. Usury diminished; credit revived. On the whole, at the end of one year, all the results predicted by Law were, for the most part, accomplished.

These fortunate beginnings secured for him the favor of the public and the entire confidence of the regent. Soon this Prince gave himself up entirely to the Scotch financier, and wished to procure him the means of putting all his plans in execution.

The first thing to do was to extend the connections of the bank and introduce its notes into the provinces, in order to change it from a special to a general bank. To accomplish this it was necessary that the notes sent into the provinces should there be converted into specie, or should be found of sufficient use to be retained there. It was this which was effected by the edict of 10th of April, 1717, given one year after the establishment of the bank. By virtue of this edict, the notes could be given in payment of duties, and the farmers of the revenue and their subordinates, the receivers, etc., in a word, all the officers of the government treasury, were ordered to give receipts for their value in specie whenever they were presented. This was the best method of aiding the general bank, since the notes sent into the provinces could be used there for the payment of taxes, or would be at once converted into specie. From this moment the banknotes were employed for all remittances from Paris to the provinces, and from the provinces to Paris.

It became useless to transport specie, for all of that which used to circulate from town to town was deposited either at the bank or the public treasuries, and exchanged for banknotes, which were transmitted in their place. In this manner the general reserved fund of the bank was likely to be increased by all the specie which its notes would displace, and Law saw himself on the point of realizing his project of a vast banking establishment, having for a reserved fund all the specie of the country. The expenses of transportation were saved, circulation was accelerated, and Law had devised a very simple means of rendering it more safe; it was to have the notes endorsed by those who sent them, the endorsement not to operate at all as a guaranty. This precaution prevented loss or theft, for the finder, or thief, could not use them. They immediately began to circulate throughout France in considerable sums. They were returned to the treasuries at Paris, covered with endorsements, and were immediately destroyed to be replaced by others.

The success of this bank was soon astonishing. With a capital of only six millions, it would issue fifty or sixty millions of notes, without confidence in it being in the slightest degree shaken. On the contrary, the demand for the notes increased every day, and the deposits of gold and silver increased perceptibly. If Law had devoted himself entirely to this institution, he would be considered one of the benefactors of our country, and the originator of a magnificent system of credit: but his impetuous nature, joined to that of the people among whom he operated, brought about, in a short time, a gigantic and disastrous imitation.

Law was now on the high road to fortune. The study of thirty years was brought to guide him in the management of his bank. He made all his notes payable at sight, and in the coin current at the time they were issued. This last was a master stroke of policy, and immediately rendered his notes more valuable than the precious metals. The latter were constantly liable to depreciation by the unwise tampering of the government. A thousand livres of silver might be worth their nominal value one day and be reduced one-sixth the next, but a note of Law's bank retained its original value. He publicly declared, at the same time, that a banker deserved death if he made issues without having sufficient security to answer all demands. The consequence was, that his notes advanced rapidly in public estimation, and were received at one percent, more than specie.

It was not long before the trade of the country felt the benefit. Languishing commerce began to lift up her head, the taxes were paid with greater regularity and less murmuring; and a degree of confidence was established that could not fail, if it continued, to become still more advantageous. In the course of a year, Law's notes rose to fifteen percent, premium, while the *billets d'etat*, or notes issued by the government as security for the debts contracted, by the extravagance of Louis XIV, were at a discount of no less than seventy-eight and a half percent.

The comparison was so greatly in favor of Law, as to attract the attention of the whole kingdom, and his credit extended itself day by day—branches of his bank were almost simultaneously established at Lyons, Rochelle, Tours, Amiens, and Orleans.

NOTES TO CHAPTER II

(1.) Financial Condition of France: During the fourteen last years of Louis XIV's reign, the expenses had absorbed two billions eight hundred millions (francs); the actual receipts had been only eight hundred and eighty millions. It was necessary to borrow about two billions in the money of that time, which is equal to about three or four billions of our money. This deficit had been consolidated in various ways, so that when the king died in September 1715, there were arrears of 711 millions; the deficit of the current year was already 78 millions. The treasury was empty. People in several provinces refused to pay taxes. As to the public distress, it is sufficient to say that great numbers died during the ensuing winter in Paris from cold and famine.—Cochet.

(2.) In the midst of this financial confusion Law appeared upon the scene. No man felt more deeply than the regent the deplorable state of the country, but no man could be more averse to putting his shoulders manfully to the wheel. He disliked business, he signed official documents without proper examination, and trusted to others what he should have undertaken himself. The cares inseparable from his high office were burdensome to him. He saw that something was necessary to be done; but he lacked the energy to do it, and had not virtue enough to sacrifice his ease and his pleasures in the attempt. No wonder that, with this character, he listened favorably to the mighty projects, so easy of execution, of the clever adventurer whom he had formerly known and whose talents he appreciated.—Mackay.

(3.) All persons whatsoever, to be at liberty to subscribe for as many shares (in Law's bank) as they pleased, and it was declared that the bank securities belonging to, as well as the money lodged in it by foreigners, should not be subject to any confiscation or attachment whatsoever, even in case of a war with the nations to which the proprietors respectively belonged. All questions to be determined by plurality of votes, those possessing from five to ten shares to have one vote; from ten to fifteen shares to have two votes, and so on in proportion; but those who had less than five shares were to be excluded from any share in the management. The accounts to be balanced twice a year, viz., from the 15th to the 20th of June, and from the 15th to the 20th of January. Two general courts to be held yearly, in which the state of the company's affairs should be discussed, and the dividends settled. The treasurer never to have more than 200,000 crowns, nor any of the cashiers more than 20,000 in hand at a time; and they were, beside, obliged to find sufficient security for their intromissions. The votes to be signed by the director, and by one of the proprietors, and to be revised by an inspector appointed by the regent. The bank not to undertake any sort of commerce whatever, nor to charge itself with the execution of any commissions; the notes to be all payable at sight, and no money to be allowed to be borrowed by the bank on any pretext whatever. Various regulations were added of less importance and too long to be enumerated in this place.—Wood.

(4.) The terms in which the notes of the General Bank were

couched, *viz*, "The bank promises to pay to the bank at sight, the sum of —— crowns, in coin of the weight and standard of this day" (of the date of each note), "value received," effectually guarded against this contingency. Let us state, by way example, that if one who had paid in, and taken out a bank note for 1,000 livres or 25 marcs, on the 2nd of June 1716, when the standard of the specie was settled by law at 40 livres the marc, wanted to exchange it at an after period when the standard was fixed at 50 livres the marc, he would, on presenting his note, receive 25 marcs or 1,250 livres. The bank was in like manner secured from suffering if the reverse took place. On this account, as well as from the quickness and punctuality of the payments, and the orders given to the officers of the revenue in all parts in the kingdom to receive the paper, without discount, in payment of taxes, the notes of the General Bank in a short time rose to great repute, and were, by many, preferred to specie, insomuch that they soon came to pass current for one percent, more than the coin itself.—Wood.

CHAPTER III

Law's scheme of a commercial company—The Mississippi Company—Jealousy of, and opposition to, Law—He is sustained by the Regent—The brothers Paris—The *anti-system*—Law initiates a speculation in stocks—Companies of the East and West Indies united—Shares rise rapidly—The Rue Quincampoix—Stockbrokers—Run on the bank—Law triumphs over everything.

CHAPTER III

Law was always scheming to concentrate into one establishment the bank, the administration of the public revenues, and the commercial monopolies. He resolved, in order to attain this end, to organize, separately, a commercial company, to which he would add, one after another, different privileges in proportion to its success, and which he would then incorporate with the general bank. Constructing thus separately each of the pieces of his vast machine, he proposed ultimately to unite them and form the grand whole, the object of his dreams and his ardent ambition.

An immense territory, discovered by a Frenchman, in the New World, presented itself for the speculations of Law. The Spanish had established themselves a long time before around the Gulf of Mexico, the English along the shores of Carolina and Virginia, the French in Canada. But, while the southern borders of America were occupied by Europeans, the interior of this beautiful country was unexplored and left to its Indian population. The Chevalier de Lasalle, the famous traveller of the time, having penetrated into America by Upper Canada, descended the river Illinois, arrived suddenly at a great river half a league wide, and, abandoning himself to the current, was borne into the Gulf of Mexico. This river was the Mississippi. The Chevalier de Lasalle took possession of the country he had passed through for the king of France, and gave it the beautiful name of Louisiana. A colony was immediately sent there. A bold trader, named Crosat, obtained the privilege of trading there, and attempted to found an establishment, which failed of success on account of the jealousy of the neighbors, the negligence of the colonists, and the want of discipline among the troops. He then demanded permission to resign this privilege, which had become a burden. Law conceived the idea of becoming his successor. There was much said of the magnificence and fertility of this new country, of the abundance of its products, of the richness of its mines, which were reported to be much more extensive than those of Mexico or Peru. Law, taking advantage of this current of opinion, projected a company which should unite the commerce of Louisiana with the fur trade of Canada. The regent granted all he asked by an edict given in August, 1717, fifteen months after the first establishment of the bank.

The new company received the title of the West Indian Company. It was to have the sovereignty of all Louisiana on the condition only of liege homage to the king of France, and of a crown of gold of thirty marcs at the commencement of every new reign. It was to exercise all the rights of sovereignty, such as levying troops, equipping vessels of war, constructing forts, establishing courts, working mines, etc. The king relinquished to it the vessels, forts and munitions of war which belonged to the Crosat Company, and conceded, furthermore, the exclusive right of the fur trade of Canada. The arms of this sovereign company represented the effigy of an old river-god leaning upon a horn of plenty.

The capital furnished by the stockholders was one hundred million francs. It was divided into two hundred thousand shares of five hundred francs each. These shares were issued in the form of a note to the holder, and were transferable by a simple endorsement. To all these arrangements Law added another very important one, with the double design of ensuring a market for the shares and of raising the national credit. We have seen that the royal stocks of all kinds had been converted into two hundred and fifty millions of state notes, which were at a discount of seventy or eighty percent, and that it was impossible to pay them from the treasury. Law caused to be inserted in the edict a clause by which the shareholders were authorized to pay one-quarter in money and three-quarters in state notes. Twenty-five millions of specie being sufficient for the first works of the company, seventy-five millions of state notes thus found an advantageous outlet, which could not fail to relieve immediately the one hundred and seventy-five millions which remained in the market. The treasury would continue to pay the four percent interest allowed on state notes, which made three millions payable annually by the state to the company. The first year these three millions were to be devoted to meeting the expenses of the first establishment of the company; the following years they were to be divided among the shareholders with the profits of the commerce. This combination had the following effect: the government abandoned to one part of its creditors the sovereignty and commerce of Louisiana and Canada, on the condition that they should advance twenty-five millions in cash toward the establishment of the new colony.

The shares of the Western Company did not, at first, produce much excitement, except among those capitalists who held state notes. The public, generally, remained indifferent, notwithstanding the marvellous things which were related of the territory which had been ceded to the company. The shares were sold below par, which was perfectly natural, as they had been paid for by twenty-five millions of money and seventy-five millions in notes, which were worth at most twenty-five millions—the whole capital then represented only fifty millions in fact, and of course the shares were below par—not unlike a good deal of our present bank capital, which is credit and credit only. However, they had contributed to raise the credit of national securities. The bank bought a certain number of them, and invested its capital of six millions in shares of the Western Company.

Law promptly commenced the initiatory steps for the establishment projected in America. Vessels were armed, troops were embarked, prostitutes and vagabonds were collected in order to send them to those solitudes which it was attempted to people. Grants of land were made, and Law rallied, even from the interior of Germany, farmers who went to Brest to embark.—(Notes 1, 2, 3.)

Law gained daily upon the esteem of the regent, a Prince passionately fond of everything ingenious and brilliant, and reduced by immediate distress to sustain himself by a mere chimera.

The Council of Finance witnessed the increasing influence of Law with jealousy, and the Duke of Noailles, president of the Council, who had always advocated economy by opposing the hazardous experiment of a system of credit, gave in his resignation. He was succeeded by M. d'Argenson, former chief of police—a bold, adroit man, devoted to the regent, but unskilled in financial matters. Law encountered still another opposition—no less than that of the parliament. This body had thought that, with an actual minority, they had yet an opportunity to recover the importance which they had lost under Louis XIV. It harassed the regent by annoyance of every description, and testified, above all, the liveliest hostility to the Scotch financier. The hatred of novelties, natural to an antiquated body, was not the only cause of this hostility. Law had said openly, that by his credit system, he would render the court independent of parliaments, by relieving them from the necessity of extraordinary taxes. He had even added that he would furnish the regent with means of repaying the expenses of the courts. To the views of strict prudence, then, were joined some entirely personal motives of hostility to Law, and they determined to fulminate a decree against his growing system.

Parliament did not know how to commence proceedings against the Western Company. There were no good reasons against the establishment of a commercial company. It decided to strike at the bank, against which, however, there was much less to say, at least in the condition in which it then was. Established in May, 1716, during a year and a half it had rendered real service to the credit of the state; having become a general bank in April, 1717, it had during five months circulated its notes throughout France. It was the decree which ordered the receipt of bank notes in payment of taxes, and which enjoined all the treasurers to pay specie for them at the demand of the holders, which parliament resolved to annul. By an act of the 18th of August, 1717, it repealed the enacting part of the decree, and forbade the receiving officers of the government to receive the notes of Law's bank.

The regent, who had many demands to make of parliament whether on the subject of the legitimate princes or on that of finances, resolved to summon them to the royal presence. The infant king was brought from Vincennes to Paris and parliament, obliged to come on foot to the Louvre, yielded to everything which the will of the regent imposed upon them. The act against the bank was annulled; it was decided, besides, that, in future, parliament's remonstrance against the royal decrees must be made within eight days, after which delay the decree should be enrolled and registered. Parliament submitted, and Law was at liberty to continue his operations. During the latter part of the year 1717 and the beginning of 1718, everything remained in *status quo*. The bank continued to render undisputed services to public and private credit, and as to the Western Company, it was making progress in establishing itself. The shares of the company rose slowly, and were still below par; but it was evident that Law, now in high favor, would soon make himself absolute master of the finances. M. d'Argenson, in his turn had become jealous of the powerful Scotchman, and he meditated an attack upon the Western Company. At this time there were three brothers engaged in commerce named Paris, well known by their vast fortune, their successful speculations, and their intimate connection with Voltaire. They were from Grenoble, shrewd, active, and universally esteemed. M. d'Argenson established a secret alliance with them, and they formed what was called the *anti-system*. The collection of one part of the public revenue was still leased, consisting of the tax on salt, on the registration of laws, on expenditures, etc., etc.; and it was these different collections united, which had been granted to an association of financiers, with the title of *Farmers General*. M. d'Argenson put them up at auction anew, and had them declared to the Paris Brothers, under the name of d'Aymard Lambert, for the annual sum of forty-eight millions five hundred thousand francs. The capital stock for this enterprise of collecting the revenues was fixed at one hundred millions, like that of the Western Company, and divided into shares of the same form and value. There was promise of large dividends on these shares, for the profits of the collections were estimated at thirteen or fourteen millions, which would make twelve or fifteen percent on the capital paid in; besides, this dividend was ensured, because it was founded, not upon the contingent successes of commerce, but upon the certain collection of the national revenues. In reality these shares were more dear, for instead of being payable in state notes, which were at seventy-five percent discount, they were payable in good securities; but their income was so great and so certain that they were sure to have the advantage over the Western shares. They obtained it, in fact, and soon they were in great demand in the market, under the name of stock in the *anti-system*.

The popularity of the bank continued constantly to increase, nevertheless; the shares of the Western Company did not rise much, but remained much below par, while the shares of the *anti-system* were very much sought. Law was not discouraged, and counted upon the achievement of his plan to triumph over the brothers Paris. At first he changed the bank from a private to a public establishment, as he had always intended to do. The 4th of December, 1718, two years and a half after its creation, it was declared to be the Royal Bank. Law was appointed director of it; the original capital was repaid to the shareholders in specie. In January, February, March and April, the increasing demand for notes caused an increase of the issue to one hundred and ten millions. They were diffused throughout France, and, to make the use of them still more universal, the transportation of coin between towns where there were offices of the bank was forbidden. The remittances between these towns must be made in banknotes. This forced measure would have been dangerous if confidence had not been absolute. It was attributable to the impatience for success which characterized the disposition of Law.—(Notes 4, 5, 6.)

Law revolved in his mind many other projects relating to his Western Company. He spoke, at first mysteriously, of the benefits which he was preparing for it. Associating with a large number of noblemen, whom his wit, his fortune, and the hope of considerable gains attracted around him, he urged them strongly to obtain for themselves some shares, which, he asserted, would soon rise rapidly in the market. He was himself soon obliged to buy some above par. The par value being five hundred francs, two hundred of them represented at par a sum of one hundred thousand francs. The price for the day being three hundred francs, sixty thousand francs was sufficient to buy two hundred shares. He contracted to pay one hundred thousand francs for two hundred shares at a fixed future time; this was to anticipate that they would gain at least two hundred francs each, and that a profit of forty thousand francs could be realized on the whole. He agreed, in order to make this sort of wager more certain, to pay the difference of forty thousand francs in advance, and to lose the difference if he did not realize a profit from the proposed transfer. This was the first instance of a sale at an anticipated advance. This kind of trade consisted in giving earnest money, called a premium, which the purchaser lost if he failed to take the property. He who made the bargain had the liberty of rescinding it if he would lose more by adhering to it than by abandoning it. No advantage would accrue to Law for the possible sacrifice of forty thousand francs, unless, at the designated time, the shares had not been worth as much as sixty thousand francs, or three hundred francs each; for having engaged to pay one hundred thousand francs for what was worth only fifty thousand, for instance, he would suffer less to lose his forty thousand francs than to keep his engagement. But, evidently, if Law did wish by this method to limit the possible loss, he hoped nevertheless not to make any loss at all; and, on the contrary, he believed firmly that the two hundred shares would be worth at least the hundred thousand francs, or five hundred francs each, at the time fixed for the expiration of the contract. This large premium attracted general attention, and people were eager to purchase the Western shares. They rose sensibly during the month of April, 1719, and went nearly to par. Law disclosed his projects; the regent kept his promise, and authorized him to unite the great commercial companies of the East and West Indies.

The two companies of the East Indies and of China, chartered in 1664 and 1713, had conducted their affairs very badly: they had ceased to carry on any commerce, and had underlet their privileges at a charge which was very burdensome to the trade. The merchants who had bought it of them did not dare to make use of their privileges, for fear that their vessels would be seized by the creditors of the company. Navigation to the East was entirely abandoned, and the necessity of reviving it had become urgent. By a decree of May, 1719, Law caused to be accorded to the West India Company the exclusive right of trading in all the seas beyond the Cape of Good Hope. From this time it had the sole right of traffic with the islands of Madagascar, Bourbon and France, the coast of Sofola in Africa, the Red Sea, Persia, Mongolia, Siam, China and Japan. The commerce of Senegal, an acquisition of the company which still carried it on, was added to the others, so that the company had the right of French trade in America, Africa and Asia. Its title, like its functions, was enlarged; it was no longer called the West Indian Company, but the Indian Company. Its regulations remained the same as before. It was authorized to issue another lot of shares, in order to raise the necessary funds either to pay the debts of the companies it succeeded or for organizing the proper establishments. Fifty thousand of these shares were issued at a par of five hundred francs, which made a nominal capital of twenty-five millions. But the company demanded five hundred and fifty francs in cash for them, or a total of twenty-seven millions two hundred and fifty thousand francs, inasmuch as it esteemed its privileges as very great and its popularity certain. It required fifty francs to be paid in advance, and the remaining five hundred in twenty equal monthly payments. In case the payments should not be fully made, the fifty francs paid in advance were forfeited by the subscriber. It was nothing but a bargain made at a premium with the public.

The prompt realization of the promises of Law, the importance and extent of the last privileges granted to the company, the facilities accorded to the subscribers, everything induced a subscription to the new shares. The movement became animated. One could, by the favorable terms offered, by paying out five hundred and fifty francs, obtain eleven shares instead of one, and thus, with a little money, speculate to a considerable amount. To this method of attracting speculators. Law added another—he procured a decision that no one should subscribe for the new shares without exhibiting four times as many old ones. It was necessary, therefore, to hasten to obtain them, in order to fulfill the requisite condition. In a short time they were carried up to par, and far above that. From three hundred francs, at which they were at the start, they rose to five hundred, five hundred and fifty, six hundred, and seven hundred and fifty francs—that is, they gained one hundred and fifty percent. These second shares were called the daughters, to distinguish them from the first.

Law, still entirely absorbed by the desire of vanquishing the *anti-system*, thought only of adding new privileges to those which the Indian Company already enjoyed. There were great profits to be made by the recoining of the specie. The reader will remember that the regent had ordered the recoining of a billion of specie, and the reissue of it for twelve hundred millions; there would be, therefore, a gain of two hundred millions. A small part of the coin had yet been brought in, and almost all the profit still remained to be made, except that which was absorbed by the counterfeiters. By a new decree of the 25th of August, 1719, Law caused to be granted to the Indian Company the coining and management of the specie. The company paid fifty millions for this new privilege. The good natured and prodigal regent needed this sum for the expenses of the government and of the court. To enable the company to pay for this, it was authorized to create fifty thousand more new shares, at five hundred francs each, which would have produced only twenty-five millions.

Nevertheless, depending upon the enthusiasm of the public, they were issued, not for five hundred and fifty francs, like the last, but for one thousand francs, in order to make up the sum due the government. The second issue of shares was called the daughters; the third was nicknamed the grand-daughters.

The same precautions were taken to ensure their success. The payments were to be made during twenty months. To procure one of the new shares it was necessary to have five of the old, and notice was given that the subscription books would be kept open only twenty days, and that after that time all the shares not subscribed for would belong to the company. These artifices, entirely novel then, produced the greatest excitement. People crowded the offices of the company to subscribe for the shares at one thousand francs. One circumstance contributed very much to excite this eagerness. The company announced that it would pay semi-annual dividends of six percent, making an annual income of twelve percent. It was possible to fulfill this promise, although it was a very bold one. There were two hundred thousand shares of the first issue, fifty thousand of the second, and fifty thousand of the third, making a total of three hundred thousand. At five hundred francs each they formed a nominal capital of one hundred and fifty millions. It required eighteen millions to make a dividend of twelve percent per annum. Now the three millions to be paid the company annually, by the government, on the seventy-five millions of state notes, the probable profit on the coinage, and the profits from commerce, might easily produce eighteen millions a year.

The month of August approached. The shares rose far above one thousand francs. Those who had bought at this price already obtained a considerable advance; but those who had purchased at five hundred, and at three hundred francs, which was the case with the first purchasers, gained one and two hundred percent profit. The creditors of the government, who had bought the first shares only to make use of their state notes, and who were rejoiced not only to recover the whole value of property which they had considered lost, but to see it doubled, hastened to sell, and to realize their unexpected profit. The speculators, more wary, held on to their shares, bought instead of sold, and thought in this way to lay the foundation of large fortunes.

There was, between the St. Denis and St. Martin, a street named the Rue Quincampoix, which had always been inhabited by bankers and brokers. There was not then at Paris, as at London and Amsterdam, an exchange, where business men assembled to trade in merchandise or public stocks. People used to go to the bankers in the Rue Quincampoix to negotiate bills and speculate in the different stocks issued by the treasury. Since the ruinous wars of Louis XIV had obliged trade to be carried on by credit, there had arisen in Paris a class of traders in notes accepted by the debtor upon whose obligations they speculated. Needy debtors produce usurers in the same way that unpunctual governments produce stockjobbers. All doubtful securities seem most to attract the venturesome speculator; he delights in such hazards, having the morality, as well as manners, of the gambler. Paris swarmed with these men, of whom some had made fortunes, while others were awaiting the opportunity to do so, and, while waiting, lived by their wits. As at this time there were no professional stockbrokers, some of these hucksters had set up counters in the Rue Quincampoix, and bought and sold the stocks in the market on others' account. Since the organization of these new companies— the Indian and that of Farmers of the Revenue—these offices were much frequented, and even the speculators, being unable to withstand this tendency, had ended by resorting to the Rue Quincampoix, where they collected in numerous groups. There, news which could affect the rise and fall of stocks was retailed, and shares were offered and sought.

There was a division among these brokers. Some pronounced themselves for Law's system, others against it. One of the most influential among them, named Leblanc, had joined the brothers Paris against Law. The Prince of Conti—who, at first, had been shown partiality in the subscriptions, but whom Law had been compelled to deny because of his exorbitant demands—had joined the opponents of what was called the *system*. They combined their means, procured a large quantity of banknotes, and demanded the specie. Law, being warned in season, paid those presented, first, and, to evade the others, he had recourse to a violent measure, which the dishonorable proceeding of his opponents accounts for without justifying. He procured a decree reducing the value of coin after a certain day. Those who hoarded specie, not wishing to submit to this reduction, hastened to deposit it in the bank. The entire public declared itself in favor of Law, and the Prince of Conti was the object of universal condemnation.

NOTES TO CHAPTER III

(1.) The regions watered by the Mississippi, immense, unknown virgin solitudes which the imagination filled with riches, was an unlimited field offered to charlatanism. The public credulity was tested with rare impudence. Large engravings were distributed representing the arrival of the French at the river, and savages with their squaws rushing to meet their new masters with evident respect and admiration. The description set forth that there were mountains filled with gold, silver, copper, lead and quicksilver. As these metals were very common and the savages did not suspect their value, they exchanged gold and silver for knives, saucepans, brooches, little looking glasses, or even a glass of brandy. One of the peculiarities of the engraving was the address to the religious. The aborigines were falling at the feet of the Jesuit priests and the legend recited that the idolatrous Indians eagerly demanded to be baptized. Great care was taken to educate their children. One old soldier named Cadillac, formerly employed in Louisiana, was so imprudent as to say that it was all humbug. His silence was secured by sending him to the Bastile.—Cochut.

(2.) Unimproved parts of Louisiana were sold for thirty thousand livres per square league.—Wood.

(3.) In order to make as much as possible out of the Mississippi, to say nothing of the jugglery practised, it was attempted to follow the example of the English, and create some efficient establishments in those vast regions. To people them, vagabonds, stout beggars, male and female, and a quantity of "public creatures" were taken from Paris and the rest of the kingdom.—Saint Simon.

(4.) 1718. The form of the notes was changed to "The bank promises to pay the bearer at sight —— livres in silver coin value received," thus making their value fluctuate with that of the coin. Law opposed this.—Wood.

(5.) After the success of the bank was established, the Duke of Orleans took it into his own hands against the wishes of Law. The General Bank was converted into the Royal Bank (1718) the king becoming responsible for the outstanding notes.—Wood.

(6.) The conversion of the General Bank into the Royal Bank the first of January 1719, was, said an excellent judge, to take away from its engagements the limited but real guaranty of an effective capital and substitute for it the indefinite and doubtful capital of a government very much involved.—Cochut.

CHAPTER IV

The national debt—Law's project for redeeming it—Caution necessary in executing the project—The collection of the revenue granted to Law's company—Arrangements for the assumption of the national debt by the company—General eagerness to subscribe for the shares—The nobility pay court to Law—Rage for speculation begins—Stock-jobbing operations of the brokers.

CHAPTER IV

Law contemplated at last the completion of his project, by uniting the collection of the revenues to the other privileges of the Indian Company, and redeeming the national debt. This was the greatest and most difficult part of his plan. Of these two measures, the first would destroy the *anti-system* and give the indirect administration of the revenues to the Indian Company; the second had been promised to the regent, and would free the government from its overwhelming burdens.

The national debt was fifteen to sixteen hundred millions, partly in contracts for perpetual annuities, partly in state notes which would soon be due. The interest on the debt was eighty millions, or one half the revenue of the government. Some combination was necessary to meet the state notes at their maturity, and to reduce the annual charges which the public treasury could no longer sustain.

Law conceived the idea of substituting the company for the government and converting the whole national debt into shares in the Indian Company. To accomplish this, he wished the company to lend the Treasury the fifteen to sixteen hundred millions which would redeem the debt; and that, to obtain this enormous sum, it should issue shares to that amount. In this manner the fifteen or sixteen hundred millions furnished to the government by the company, and paid out by the government to its creditors, must return to the company by the sale of its shares. Let us see the means which Law had devised to ensure the success of his scheme. The government would pay three percent, interest for the sum loaned to it, which would make forty-five or forty-eight millions a year. The treasury would thus effect an annual saving of thirty-two or thirty-five millions in the interest on the debt. In return, the collection of the revenue must be transferred to the company, notwithstanding that it had been actually granted to the brothers Paris. The collection would pay the collectors a net profit of fifteen or sixteen millions. The company, receiving three percent, interest on the capital invested, and reaping from another source a profit of fifteen or sixteen millions, would be in a position to pay four percent, on the sixteen hundred millions of the debt converted into shares.

The profits from commerce and its future success might soon enable it to increase this dividend. According to the prevailing rates of interest, which had fallen to three percent, since the establishment of the bank, this was a sufficient remuneration on the shares. They had, beside, the hope of increasing their capital. The shares having, in fact, doubled in value during the opposition of the *anti-system*, they ought to increase still more rapidly since they were relieved from this opposition. The expectation that the fifteen or sixteen hundred millions of the debt would be invested in the shares was well founded. There was even a certainty of it; for this immense capital, forcibly expelled from its investment in state securities, could find no other place for investment than in the company.

This plan of Law was vast and bold. Its success would liquidate the state debt and diminish the annual charges on the treasury, reducing the interest from eighty millions to forty-five or forty-eight millions. The annual charges, from which the treasury was to be relieved, were to be paid from the profits on the collection of the revenue, and the contingent profits of commerce. The whole operation was to pay the creditors of the state three percent, per annum, and the profits and monopolies heretofore granted to farmers of the revenue and commercial companies. This three percent, interest, these profits, and these monopolies, as we shall soon see, might easily amount to the sum of eighty millions annually which the creditors were formerly paid. Thus far they were not defrauded by this forced conversion of securities; a credit entirely new was substituted for one which was worn out; an establishment had been created, which, combining the functions of a commercial bank and the administration of the finances, must become the most colossal financial power ever known.

But if this plan offered some indisputable advantages, yet the wisest precautions were necessary in the execution of it. In fact, fifteen or sixteen hundred millions suddenly displaced and transferred from the state securities to shares in the Indian Company must be managed with extreme prudence to induce these millions to come to the company, and at the same time to prevent all precipitation; to avoid either reluctance or a too great eagerness to buy. We shall see what measures were taken to accomplish this operation, the most audacious that had ever been attempted in finance.

By a decree of the 27th of August, 1719, the lease of the principal revenues was cancelled. They were withdrawn from the brothers Paris and granted to the Indian Company, who, instead of forty-five millions five hundred thousand francs a year, agreed to pay into the treasury fifty-two millions a year. The company promised to lend the government fifteen hundred millions, at three percent; this made, consequently, forty-five millions due the company annually, which it was authorized to deduct from the products of the revenue, so that there only remained seven millions a year to be paid to the government.

The payment of the different securities was then ordered, each in its separate order. The holders of the different titles were invited to present themselves at the offices of the treasury, where receipts would be given them for the value of their claims, which receipts they would then present at the offices of the company who would pay the amount of them in specie or in banknotes. It had been agreed that a sufficient quantity of notes should be manufactured to make these payments, and that they should be destroyed immediately when they were received back in payment for the shares. The payment of the debt must inevitably be effected before it could be converted into shares of the Indian Company. It was therefore necessary to make the advance. The bank, now a royal institution, was commissioned to accomplish this by its notes.

Scarcely were these arrangements made public, when an extraordinary animation was everywhere manifested. The shares of the farmers of the revenue and the state notes being about to disappear, the shares of the Indian Company would be the only ones remaining for the speculators; besides, as the debt was to be paid, it was evident that they offered an investment which would be eagerly sought. They rose with singular rapidity. From one thousand and fifteen hundred francs each, they rose to two, three, and four thousand francs; that is, to four, six, and eight times the original cost.—(Note 1.)

On the 13th of September, Law commenced the issue of the new shares. There were already three hundred thousand shares of a capital of one hundred and fifty millions—some issued at five hundred francs, others at five hundred and fifty, and the last at one thousand. A new issue of one hundred thousand shares was ordered, at the nominal price of five hundred francs, and at a realized price of five thousand francs, which made a nominal capital of fifty millions and a fund paid in of five hundred millions. It was a third of the sum which the company

CHAPTER IV

was bound to furnish the government. The payment was to be made in ten equal installments, payable monthly. The first was the only one demanded in cash.

The eagerness to subscribe was prodigious. All the disposable capital, whether in the hands of the brokers or in those of the creditors of the state, was invested in the subscriptions. Everyone foresaw the importance of those shares, which were to be the sole investment for the fifteen hundred millions, divided previously in the public debt into different kinds of stock, and people rushed to secure them early, in order to make the unfortunate state creditors pay dear for them. The acquisition of them in large amounts was not difficult, as with five thousand francs, ten shares could be subscribed for.—(Note 2.)

The creditors, seeing themselves deprived of their investment, complained, with reason, that they had not the preference over every other class of subscribers. Law, perceiving the mistake he had made, procured a decree the 26th of September, thirteen days after the opening of the subscription books, ordering the payment for the shares to be received only in state notes or in receipts. This ensured the creditors the preference, or, what was as well, an advantageous sale of their securities to speculators. But this was done rather late, as the speculators had already secured to themselves a large part of the amount issued. This measure, although tardy, had still another advantage. It relieved the treasury from paying the advance on the redemption of the debt in banknotes. Instead of exchanging the receipts for notes and the notes for shares, the receipts were taken directly to the office for receiving subscriptions. The proceeding was thus simplified, and the transient issue of an enormous number of notes was avoided.

The first subscription having been taken up in a few days, Law opened a new one on the 28th of September, for the same amount and on exactly the same conditions as the preceding.

The eagerness of subscribers was the same. The creditors passed whole days at the offices of the treasury to obtain their receipts, and there were some even who had their meals brought to them there, so that they might not lose their turn in the ranks. The state notes were, of course, much in demand, and had rapidly risen to par. They had even given rise to a most reprehensible speculation. A confidential clerk of Law, the Prussian Versinobre, having known in advance of the decree regarding the payment, abused his knowledge of the secret, and caused to be bought by brokers with whom he was associated, a large amount of state notes at fifty or sixty percent below their nominal value, and employed them for the subscriptions when they were received at par. When it is considered that the subscriptions, already, were sold at a large advance, and that by means of the state notes they were bought at about half price, it will be understood what a profit this company of brokers must have realized.

Those who intended to subscribe had accomplished comparatively little by obtaining receipts or state notes; it was still necessary to go to the Hôtel de Nevers, where the subscriptions were received. The entrances there were crowded to suffocation. The hall servants made considerable sums by subscribing for those who could not get through the crowd to the offices. Some adventurers, assuming the livery of Law, performed this service, charging and obtaining a very large fee. The most humble employees of the company became patrons who were very much courted. As to the higher officers, and Law himself, they received as much adulation as if they were the actual dispensers of the favors of fortune. The approaches to Law's residence were encumbered with carriages. All that was most brilliant among the nobility of France came to beg humbly for the subscriptions, which were already much above the nominal price of shares, and which were sure to rise much

CHAPTER IV 59

higher. By a clause of the decree creating the company, the ownership of the shares entailed nothing derogatory to rank. The nobility, therefore, could indulge in this speculation without endangering its titles. It was as much in debt as the king, thanks to its prodigality and the long wars of that century, and it sought to win, at least, the amount of its debts by fortunate speculations. It surrounded, it fawned upon Law, who, very anxious to gain partisans, reserved very few shares for himself, but distributed them among his friends of the court.—(Note 4.)

The new subscription was also taken up in a few days. If we reflect that fifty millions in cash was sufficient to secure five hundred millions of each issue, we shall understand how the state notes which remained in the market, and the receipts already delivered, would suffice to monopolize the shares offered to the public. The creditors who had not liquidated their claims, and the greater number had not, could not avail themselves of the right to subscribe for shares, and were obliged to buy them in the market at an exorbitant price. The shares subscribed for at the Hôtel de Nevers for five thousand francs, were resold in the Rue Quincampoix for six, seven, and eight thousand francs. To the need of having some of this investment, was joined the hope of seeing the shares rise in the market to an indefinite extent, and it is not surprising that the eagerness to obtain them soon increased to frenzy. In order to satisfy this demand, a third subscription was opened on the second of October, three days after the second. Similar in every respect to the first two, it ought to bring in a capital of five hundred millions and complete the fifteen hundred millions which the company needed to redeem the public debt.

The concourse of people was as great as ever at the treasury where the receipts were given, and at the Hôtel de Nevers, where the applications for shares were received. The occasion of this eagerness is evident, since that which was obtained at the Hôtel de Nevers for five thousand francs was worth seven and eight thousand in the Rue Quincampoix. This new issue at five thousand francs caused the rates in the Rue Quincampoix to diminish; in an instant they were below five thousand francs—even as low as four thousand—so blind were these movements, and, so to speak, convulsive, during this period of feverish excitement. There was no possible reason for selling in one place for four thousand francs, that for which they paid five thousand at another. But this phenomenon lasted only a few hours; the rates rose again rapidly, and the subscription being taken up, the shares sold again for seven and eight thousand francs. The crafty brokers had already had two opportunities of making some profitable operations.

Having obtained the state notes at a very small price, they procured shares at the most moderate rates, between five hundred and a thousand francs; then they sold them for from seven to eight thousand francs; and on the 2nd of October, the day of the decline, they repurchased them for four thousand, to sell them again the next day for seven or eight thousand. It will be seen how they must have made money, with these opportunities.

It was no longer a few scattered groups which were seen in the Rue Quincampoix, but a compact crowd engaged in speculating from morning till night. The subscriptions had been divided into coupons, transferable, like notes, to the bearer by an endorsement simply formal. During the course of October the shares had already risen above ten thousand francs, and it was impossible to know where they would stop.—(Note 3.)

NOTES TO CHAPTER IV

(1.) It was now that the frenzy of speculating began to seize upon the nation. Law's bank had effected so much good, that any promises for the future which he thought proper to make were readily believed. The regent every day conferred new privileges upon the fortunate projector. The bank obtained the monopoly of the sale of tobacco, the sole right of refining gold and silver, and was finally erected into the Royal Bank of France. Amid the intoxication of success, both Law and the regent forgot the maxim so loudly proclaimed by the former, that a banker deserved death who made issues of paper without the necessary funds to provide for them. As soon as the bank, from a private, became a public institution, the regent caused a fabrication of notes to the amount of one thousand millions of livres. This was the first departure from sound principles, and one for which Law is not justly blamable. While the affairs of the bank were under his control, the issues had never exceeded sixty millions. Whether Law opposed this inordinate increase is not known; but, as it took place as soon as the bank was made a royal establishment, it is but fair to lay the blame of change of system upon the regent.—Mackay.

(2.) The public enthusiasm, which had been so long rising, could not resist a vision so splendid. At least three hundred thousand applications were made for the fifty thousand new shares, and Law's house in the rue de Quincampoix was beset from morning to night by the eager applicants.—Mackay.

(3.) The situation of France, in November, 1719, is thus described by a contemporary writer: "The bank notes were just so much real value which credit and confidence had created in favor of the state. Upon their appearance, plenty immediately displayed herself through all the towns and all the country; she relieved our citizens and laborers from the oppression of debts which indigence had obliged them to contract; she enabled the king to liberate himself from great part of his debts, and to make over to his subjects more than fifty-two millions of livres of taxes which had been imposed in the years preceding 1719; and more than thirty-five millions of other duties extinguished during the regency. This plenty sunk the rate of interest, crushed the usurer, carried the value of lands to 80 and 100 years' purchase, raised up stately edifices both in town and country, repaired the old houses which were falling to ruin, improved the soil, gave an additional relish to every fruit produced by the earth. Plenty recalled those citizens whom misery had forced to seek their livelihood abroad. In a word, riches flowed in from every quarter; gold, silver, precious stones, ornaments of every kind which contribute to luxury and magnificence, came to us from every country in Europe. Whether these prodigies or marvellous effects were produced by art, by confidence, by fear, or by whim, if you please, one must agree, that that art, that confidence, that fear, or that whim, had operated all these realities, which the ancient administration never could have produced. Thus far the system had produced nothing but good; everything was commendable and worthy of admiration."—Wood.

(4.) To the eyes of the wondering crowd, the author of

such prodigies was, during some time, a chimerical being, superhuman, a demigod in whose honor a sort of worship was cultivated. The Academy of Science elected him one of its members. As he passed through the streets people cried, "Long live the king and Monseigneur Law!" He was overwhelmed with supplicating flatteries in prose and verse. His very servants were courted, and gentlemen assumed his livery to introduce themselves into the bank or to have more credit in the Rue Quincampoix. Women, sad to relate, distinguished themselves by their adulations and baseness. The regent's mother wrote to a friend that "Law was so beset that he had no repose, night or day. A duchess kissed his hand before a crowd of people. If a duchess will kiss his hand, what will not other women kiss?" Like Midas, whose touch converted everything into gold and almost caused him to die of hunger, the financier no longer had time to live. Badgered in every saloon where he showed himself, pursued in the streets, tracked to his private apartments by women who intruded themselves by force or by fraud, and waited day and night till they met their victim, poor Law saw countesses and marquesses ready to spring upon him at times when decency even required a solitary retirement.—Cochut.

CHAPTER V

Mistake in the details of the execution of Law's project—New privileges granted to the company—Speculation attracts all classes and affects all kinds of business—Foreigners arrive—Tricks of the brokers—Fortunes made in a few hours—Actual value of the shares—Law becomes idolized—Anecdotes—His conversion—Courted by foreign governments—Continued success of the bank—Excessive luxury of speculators—Income of the company.

CHAPTER V

Few explanations are necessary to expose the mistake committed by Law in the execution of his project. Nothing was more admissible or more practicable than the conversion of the whole capital of the public debt from one kind of stock to another. The state might make a saving by doing so, and the creditors could lose nothing; but the greatest precautions were necessary to accomplish this conversion without confusion or disorder. Unfortunately none of these precautions were taken, and we are overwhelmed with astonishment at the manner in which Law conducted this important operation. He had first advertised the redemption of the public debt by the Indian Company; he had suffered the shares to rise as high as five thousand francs, so that the holders of the first made ten to one on their capital, and what they obtained for five hundred and a thousand francs the creditors of the state paid five thousand for. He had then decided to open new subscriptions, and opened them before the creditors had taken their receipts, and consequently before their securities were in a disposable form. He had then granted such terms that those who were most alert had the advantage of the others, and one hundred and fifty millions sufficed to engross the stock of fifteen hundred millions. Then Law had offered the subscriptions at three different times, as if he wished to stimulate the eagerness to buy by satisfying it only little by little.

With such management it was natural that the subscriptions should be snatched at, and that the movement, which should have been quiet and steady, became precipitate and violent.

The precautions which ought to have been taken are obvious. The shares should not have been suffered to rise to five thousand francs, for this permitted the holders of the first shares to make an unfair profit at the expense of the creditors of the state. The subsequent subscriptions should not have been opened before all the receipts had been delivered, so that not one of the creditors should have cause to complain. It should have been declared also, on the first day, that receipts and state notes alone would be received in payment for shares, so that speculators who had none of the public debt should not have the power of taking shares without first purchasing securities from the actual creditors of the state. Lastly, in order to give all the creditors an opportunity to subscribe, the right of paying by installments should not have been granted; this would have prevented the fifteen hundred millions of stock being taken up with one hundred and fifty millions of capital.

None of these precautions were taken, as we have just seen. The reason assigned for granting the right of payment by installments was that the claims of creditors could not all be liquidated immediately—it must be done gradually. This reason would have been sound if each creditor paying for his shares by installments of one-tenth, according to the terms of subscriptions, had received his receipts in the same proportion. But each creditor received the whole of his claim at once, and thus the first comer had an advantage. Beside, the state notes, all transferable and in the market, had an immense advantage over the receipts, which occasioned, as we have seen, some fraudulent transactions. The requirement that the payment should be made in receipts, or in state notes, was offered in excuse, because it must sooner or later bring the shares or their value into the hands of the creditors, since the subscribers would be compelled to buy the receipts of the creditors at a price proportionate to the price of the shares, or to abandon the shares to them at a reduced rate for want of the necessary paper to purchase with. This would be a good excuse if the provision had been adopted the first day; but when it was thought of, a disordered movement was already produced in the price of the shares, and there was no means either of arresting or moderating the agitation.

None of these much-needed precautions were taken. Law, absorbed by the obstacle to be overcome in order to ensure the success of his plan, aimed only to dazzle the world by a prodigious success, and had done everything to stimulate subscribers, instead of doing everything to restrain them.

This dangerous success went on constantly increasing to the end of October and beginning of November of 1719. Law, carried away as much as the public, neglected nothing to enlarge the functions of the company. He had the revenue on tobacco assigned to the company for one hundred millions in addition to what it had lent to government, and which served to redeem four millions of pensions secured upon this revenue. The company receiving only three percent, or three millions, it was a saving of a million to the government. The regent took the occasion of this economy to abolish the duties on tallow, oil, fish, etc., which gave great joy to the people of Paris and singularly increased the popularity of the system.

It was no longer only the professional speculators and creditors of the government who frequented the Rue Quincampoix, all classes of society mingled there, cherishing the same illusions—noblemen, famous on the field of battle, distinguished in the government—churchmen, traders, quiet citizens, servants whom their suddenly acquired fortune had filled with the hope of rivalling their masters. All the houses in the street had been converted into offices by the stockjobbers; the occupants gave up their apartments, the merchants their shops; houses which had brought a rent of seven or eight hundred francs were cut up into some thirty offices, and brought fifty or sixty thousand francs; stock-jobbing made itself felt in rents as in securities. A cobbler who had converted his stall into an office by placing in it some stools, a table and a writing-desk, rented it for two hundred francs a day.—(Notes 4, 5-10.)

The shops had been changed into cafés and restaurants; a portion of the Parisians had almost transferred their residences to this quarter; they came there at daybreak, breakfasted there, dined there, and, when the fever of speculation had subsided, passed the afternoon at cards. Numerous equipages, awaiting their owners, obstructed the streets of St. Denis and St. Martin, parallel to the Rue Quincampoix.

A large number of provincials and foreigners were added to the population of Paris, especially those from the important cities of Europe. Many did not dare to operate for themselves, either from timidity or from want of experience, and they employed the intrepid brokers formed under the last reign to operate for them. These brokers had organized themselves into regular swindling companies. They speculated upon the constant rise, but more often still upon the fluctuations which they had the skill to produce. They arranged themselves in a line in the Rue Quincampoix, ready to act at the first signal. At the sound of a bell in the office of a man named Papillon, they offered, all at once, the shares, sold them, and effected a decline. At a different signal, they bought at the lowest price that which they had sold at the highest, and in this way brought about a reaction; thus they always "sold dear and bought cheap." The fluctuations were so rapid and so considerable, that brokers receiving shares to sell had time to make large profits by retaining them only one day. One is mentioned who, commissioned to sell some shares, was absent two days. It was thought that he had stolen them. Not at all; he repaid the price of them faithfully, but meanwhile he had made a million for himself.

This power which capital had acquired of realizing such quick profits, had originated a special business. Money was lent by the hour and at an unexampled interest. The stockjobbers not only found means to pay the interest demanded, but also made notable profits for themselves. A million francs were sometimes made in one day. It is not astonishing, then, that servants became suddenly as rich as their masters. One of them, meeting his master walking in the rain, stopped his carriage to offer him a seat.

The Rue Quincampoix was called the *Mississippi*. Every day industrious mechanics and quiet gentlemen abandoned their labor or the enjoyment of their peaceable competency to embark on this tempestuous sea. Their number constantly increased, and in November all were under the fascination of this wild illusion. At this time the shares were quoted at fifteen thousand francs, or thirty times the original price. No one stopped to ask what was the foundation of this enormous wealth; no one reflected that paper had no value, except as representing realities, and that the shares really represented the values shown overleaf:

Values Represented by the Shares

100,000,000	francs for the first issue of shares to the number of	200,000
27,500,000	francs for the second issue of shares to the number of	50,000
50,000,000	francs for the third issue of shares to the number of	50,000
1,500,000,000	francs for the last issue of shares to the number of	300,000
1,677,500,000	francs for the four issues, making a total of	600,000

While the six hundred thousand shares represented, in fact, the sum of one billion six hundred and seventy-seven million five hundred thousand francs, they had risen, at the price of fifteen thousand francs, to represent a sum amounting to nine billons. Had the commerce of all the Indies ever produced profits to justify such a rise in the capital and to pay a proportionate interest? Had it, for example, produced four hundred and fifty millions in a year, so as to have paid five percent, at least, upon the capital so suddenly created? No one asked himself these questions. Every one seemed to think, with Law, that all wealth was in money; that paper could take the place of it, and that the shares were really worth their market price. —(Note 12 records the number and value of shares issued by the company.)

Law was idolized. The nobility filled his antechambers. One of his old friends, being in his private apartments, saw him go through some long calculations, breakfast, then play at faro, While a crowd of noblemen patiently waited for him. There was no insolence in this; but he could not have attended to the indispensable duties of life if he had yielded to the universal enthusiasm for him. A lady had her carriage overturned beneath his windows to compel him to show himself. Law had lost none of his original modesty; but his wife, less intelligent than he, could not conceal the self-conceit of a *parvenue*, and manifested impertinently the annoyance which the assiduities of her flatterers occasioned her. The son of Law was admitted to dine with the king, who was the same age; his daughter, scarcely eight years old, gave a ball at her house. The most brilliant of the nobility sued for the honor of an invitation to this *fête* given by a child. The papal nuncio arrived among the first, seized the young mistress of the house in his arms, and overwhelmed her with caresses. Dukes and princes sought the hand of this little girl, scarcely out of the cradle.—(Notes 3, 7, 8, 9.)

The regent, charmed like every one else, removed M. d'Argenson from the Treasury to give it to Law. He being, a protestant, the Abbé de Tencin was commissioned to convert him. The neighboring governments could not but feel some disquietude at the apparent financial power and strength of France. England wished to temporize with Law, who had retained a lively resentment against his own country. The impetuous Stair, the English ambassador, who had offended Law, was recalled. Facts like these show the influence which Law commanded in France and in Europe. It appears that, notwithstanding the superiority of his intelligence, he himself shared the general intoxication. He purchased estates in France, took no precaution to secure a fortune abroad, and there is nothing to indicate that he foresaw his sad approaching fate.—(Notes 1, 2, 4.)

While the shares of the company rose so high, the notes of the bank had no less success. The bank remained still separate from the company. The convenience of the notes in the quick transactions of the Rue Quincampoix, made them very much in demand. Large amounts of gold and silver were deposited to procure them, and they had even come to be worth ten percent more than coin. The bank had been obliged to issue as much as six hundred and forty millions at a time. However, they were not so generally diffused through the provinces as at Paris, because they were not needed there for stock-jobbing transactions. Law wished to supply what was wanting to their success in the provinces by a decree of the 1st of December, 1719, by which the conversion of gold and silver into banknotes was forbidden in Paris and authorized in the provinces alone. The revenue also must be paid in banknotes, and creditors were empowered to insist upon payment in the same form. The intention of the edict is apparent; the issue of notes being arrested in Paris, where it had become excessive, the source from which they were obtained was transported to the provinces: beside, the collection of the taxes in notes and the power given to creditors to demand payment in that money must contribute to expand their circulation to the remotest extremities of the country. It is true that the circulation of the notes was not forced, for that would have required every one to receive them; but as they were worth more than specie, the authorizing of everybody to demand them was to oblige everybody to have them. Thus Law already adopted forced measures to extend the success of the bank into the provinces.

The month of December was the time of the greatest infatuation. The shares ended by rising to eighteen and twenty thousand francs—thirty-six and forty times the first price. Everything had been systematized in the Rue Quincampoix. Guards were placed at both extremities of the street; a commission had been appointed to settle all disputes summarily. The concourse of speculators constantly increased. People from every quarter rushed to this general rendezvous of fortune. Creditors brought the sums received from their debtors; proprietors brought the value of their estates, and

CHAPTER V

ladies that of their diamonds. The *Mississippians* began to abandon themselves to the pleasures and dissipations which attend suddenly acquired fortunes. The regent freed from his cares, the nobility believing itself wealthy, the brokers possessing immense quantities of paper, indulged in every kind of debauchery. The shops in the rue St. Honoré, commonly filled with the richest stuffs, were emptied; the cloth of gold had become extremely scarce—it was seen in the streets worn by all sorts of people. An unheard-of number of equipages paraded the capital; the streets St. Denis and St. Martin, contiguous to the Rue Quincampoix, were so blocked up by the carriages of rich *Mississippians* that the merchants complained to the regent that they seriously interfered with their trade.—(Notes 6, 11.)

So unnatural a state of things could not last long. Before Law had made his system complete, before he had given the company the last privileges he had designed for it, and had united it with the bank, the shares were to suffer a frightful decline. At the price they had attained, the six hundred thousand shares represented a capital of ten or twelve billions. The only means of sustaining this absurd fiction would have been to pay a proportionate interest to the shareholders, and four or five millions of income would have been required to ensure four percent only. The income of the company was as follows:

Amount and Origin of Company Income

From the collection of the national revenue for the interest on 1,600,000,000, of the public debt	48,000,000
Profits on farming the revenue	15,000,000
Profits on the general receipts	1,500,000
Profits on tobacco	2,000,000
Profits on coining the money	4,000,000

Profits from commerce	10,000,000
Total	80,500,000

This income would have allowed a dividend of five percent at most upon the actual capital of one billion six hundred and seventy-seven millions. How was it possible to provide even a moderate income for a capital of ten billions, and thus to give it some reality?

The exaggeration of the price must cease at the moment when the fiction was contrasted with facts, and this would be when the shareholders attempted to realize their fortune, whether to ensure it or to enjoy it.

NOTES TO CHAPTER V

(1.) Law was now made comptroller general of the finances, precisely at the time when it was impossible that he could fill the duties of the position; at the period of the subversion of private fortunes and the public finances. People saw him converted in a short time from a Scotchman to a naturalized Frenchman, from a Protestant to a Catholic, from a needy adventurer to a lord of magnificent estates, from a banker to a minister of state. I have seen him arrive in the saloons of the Palais Royal followed by dukes, lords, marshals of France and bishops. At last, in the same year, Law, loaded with public execration, was compelled to fly the country which he had wished to enrich and in which he had produced such disorders.—Voltaire.

(2.) At this time he was by far the most influential person of the state. The Duke of Orleans had so much confidence in his sagacity and the success of his plans, that he always consulted him upon every matter of moment. He was by no means unduly elevated by his prosperity, but remained the same simple, affable, sensible man that he had shown himself in adversity. His gallantry, which was always delightful to the fair objects of it, was of a nature so kind, so gentlemanly, and so respectful, that not even a lover could have taken offence at it. If, upon any occasion, he showed any symptoms of haughtiness, it was to the cringing nobles who lavished their adulation upon him till it became fulsome. He often took pleasure in seeing how long he could make them dance attendance upon him for a single favor. To such of his own countrymen as by chance visited Paris, and sought an interview with him, he was; on the contrary, all politeness and attention.—Mackay.

(3.) Peers, whose dignity would have been outraged if the regent had made them wait half an hour for an interview, were contented to wait six hours for the chance of seeing Monsieur Law. Enormous fees were, paid to his servants, if they would merely announce their names. Ladies of rank employed the blandishment of their smiles for the same object; but many of them came day after day for a fortnight before they could obtain an audience. When Law accepted an invitation, he was sometimes so surrounded by ladies, all asking to have their names put down in his lists as shareholders in the new stock, that, in spite of his well-known and habitual gallantry, he was obliged to tear himself away *par force*.—Mackay.

(4.) A British nobleman, who then visited Paris, said, in a public advertisement, that Mr. Law appeared a minister far above all the past age had known, the present could conceive, or the future could believe; that he had established public credit in a country that was become a proverb for the breach of it; and that he had shown the French people that Louis XIV was not able, with his unlimited authority, to take away more from, than he had restored to them. Madame de la Chaumont having been detected in illicit practices against the revenue, was drawn out of the scrape by the exertions of one of the contractors for supplying the French army with provisions. This acceptable piece of service led her to support their interest with so much warmth, that she soon found herself engaged for them in the sum of 1,400,000 livres, advanced by herself, and borrowed from her relations and neighbors. Coming from Paris to solicit payment, she was forced to accept that sum in *billets d'etat*, although they were then at sixty percent discount. Unwilling to return to Namur with less than would satisfy her creditors, and resolving to risk everything to accomplish that object, she laid out the whole in the purchase of shares of the India Company immediately on its institution, which happened just at that period, and, consequently, became enriched beyond her utmost expectations.

Mr. Chiral, principal physician to the regent, on his way to visit a female patient, having been informed that the price of actions was falling, was so affected by that piece of news that he could think of nothing else; and, accordingly, while holding the lady's pulse, kept exclaiming, "O good God! it falls, it falls!" The invalid, naturally alarmed, began to ring the bell with all her force, crying out that she was a dead woman, and had almost expired with apprehension, till the doctor assured her that her pulse was in a very good state, but that his mind was so much upon actions, that he came to utter the expression that terrified her in reference to the fall of their value. That learning herself could not shield her votaries from the infection, appears from the following circumstance: M. de la Motte and the Abbé Terrasson, two of the ablest scholars in France, conversing together on the madness of the Mississippi adventurers, congratulated themselves on their superiority over all weaknesses of that nature; and indulged themselves in ridiculing the folly of the votaries of the fickle goddess. But it so happened that they met, not long afterward, face-to-face in the Rue Quincampoix; at first, they endeavored to avoid each other, but, finding that impracticable, put the best look possible to the matter, rallied each other, and separated in order to make the most advantageous bargains they could.—Wood.

(5.) The memoirs of the regency (vol. ii. p. 331) contain a notice of a hump-backed man, who in the course of a few days acquired 150,000 livres by letting out his hump as a writing desk to the brokers in the Rue Quincampoix. A plan of Paris being about this time laid before Louis XV, then only ten years of age, the young monarch found fault with it, because that street (Rue Quincampoix), was not distinguished from the others by gilding.—Wood.

(6.) A footman had gained so much that he provided himself with a fine carriage; but the first day it came to the door, he, instead of stepping into the vehicle, mounted up to his old station behind. Another, in a similar predicament, brought himself well off by pretending he got up only to see if there was room on the back for two or three more lackeys, whom he was resolved to hire instantly. Mr. Law's coachman had made so great a fortune that he asked to be dismissed from his service, which was readily granted, on condition of procuring another as good as himself. The man thereupon brought two coachmen to his master, they were both excellent drivers, and desired him to make choice of one, at the same time saying that he would take the other for his own carriage. One night at the opera, a Mademoiselle de Begond, observing a lady enter magnificently dressed, and covered with diamonds, jogged her mother, and said, "I am much mistaken if this fine lady is not Mary, our cook." The report spread through the theatre, till it came to the ears of the lady, who, coming up to Madame de Begond, said, "I am indeed Mary your cook, I have gained large sums in the Rue Quincampoix. I love fine clothes and fine jewels, and am accordingly dressed in them. I have paid for everything, am in debt to nobody, and pray what has any person in this place to say to this?" At another time, some persons of quality beholding a gorgeous figure alight from a most splendid equipage, and inquiring what great lady that was, one of her lackeys answered, "A woman who has tumbled from a garret into a carriage." One of these upstarts, finding himself enriched beyond his utmost expectations, hastened to a coachmaker's and ordered a berlin to be made in the finest taste, lined with the richest crimson velvet and gold fringe, and went away after leaving 4,000 livres as earnest. The coachmaker running after him to inquire what arms were to be put on the carriage, was answered, "Oh, *the finest—the finest* by all means." A quondam footman sitting in a newly acquired carriage, having his way impeded by another belonging to an officer, their servants quarrelled, and the former having made use of some improper expressions, the officer obliged him to alight and putting his hand to his sword, the other took to his heels, crying out, "Brethren of the livery, come to my assistance."

But, perhaps, the drollest circumstance that occurred, was what happened to one Brignaud (son of a baker at Toulouse), who being desirous of having a superb service of plate, purchased the whole articles exposed for sale in the shop of a goldsmith for 400,000 livres, and sent them home to his wife, with orders to set them out properly for supper, to which he had invited many persons of distinction. The lady, not understanding the business, arranged the plate according to her fancy, and without regard to their real use; so that when supper was announced the guests could not forbear from indulging in peals of laughter to see the soup served up in a basin for receiving the offerings at church, the sugar in a censer, and chalices holding the place of salt-cellars, while most of the other articles were more suited to a toilet than a sideboard.—Wood.

(7.) An old lady who wished to obtain the concession of some shares from Law after the subscription was closed, said in her eagerness, "*Faites moi une conception,*" (she meant to ask for a 'concession' but actually asked for a 'conception'). Law replied, *"Vous venez trop tard, il n'y a pas moyen à présent"* (You come too late, it is no longer possible.)—Wood.

(8.) Someone directed another, who was inquiring for a certain duchess, to Law's house, where all the duchesses were sure to be assembled.—Wood.

(9.) Law was not exalted by the excessive adulation he received; he was simple and unostentatious in his style and habits.—Wood.

(10.) It may, perhaps, require some explanation how so many low persons should acquire large fortunes from nothing, in so short a time; but, independent of the rise in the price of actions, various, indeed, were the ways of doing so during the Mississippi contagion. Some, either unable or unwilling to go to the Rue Quincampoix to dispose of their shares, trusted them to others, who received orders to sell for a certain sum. On their arrival, they commonly found the price risen, and without scruple put the price in their own pockets. A gentleman, falling sick, sent his servant to dispose of 250 shares for 8,000 livres each; and he sold them at the rate of 10,000 livres, making a profit of 500,000 livres, which he appropriated to himself, and, by other lucky adventures, increased that sum to upwards of two millions. A person deputed to sell 200 shares for another, kept himself concealed for some days, during which time their price rose so high that he cleared near a million of livres of profit, giving back to his employer, who had been hunting him in vain, only the market rate of the day on which he was sent to dispose of the actions. One De Josier, trusted with the like number of shares to sell for 550 livres each, disappeared, but coming back when the system was at its height, profited immensely.—Wood.

(11.) The honest old soldier, Marshal Villars, was so vexed to see the folly which had smitten his countrymen, that he never could speak with temper on the subject. Passing one day through the Place Vendôme in his carriage, the choleric gentleman was so annoyed at the infatuation of the people, that he abruptly ordered his coachman to stop, and, putting his head out of the carriage window, harangued them for full half an hour on their "disgusting avarice." This was not a very wise proceeding on his part. Hisses and shouts of laughter resounded from every side, and jokes without number were aimed at him. There being at last strong symptoms that something more tangible was flying through the air in the direction of his head, the marshal was glad to drive on. He never again repeated the experiment.—Mackay's *Popular Delusions.*

(12.) Number and Value of Shares Issued by the Company of the Indies.

Successive emissions	Number of shares	Nominal price of shares	Total price	Actual price per share	Actual price of each emission
1st Capital	200,000	500	100,000,000	500	100,000,000
1st Subscription	50,000	500	25,000,000	500	27,500,000
2nd Subscription	50,000	500	25,000,000	1,000	50,000,000
3rd Subscription	300,000	500	150,000,000	5,000	1,500,000,000
Supplementary	24,000	500	12,000,000	5,000	120,000,000
	624,000		312,000,000		1,797,500,000

Thus the company had issued 624,000 shares at 500 francs each, representing 312 million francs, but profiting by the rise they had sold them for 1,797,500,000 francs. For paying a dividend upon this enormous sum, their total probable receipts were 82,000,000, which would have given 130 francs upon a share of 500 francs, a magnificent result. But it is to be observed that the greater part of the subscribers had paid 5,000 francs for their shares and to give a dividend of four percent per annum it was necessary to make a dividend of 200 francs per share.—Cochut.

CHAPTER VI

Extravagant prices of goods—First decline of shares—Drain of specie from the bank—Forced measures resorted to—Attempts to revive confidence by adding new functions to the company—*Letter to a Creditor*—Panic increases—Odious measures—Licentiousness of the realizers—Banknotes might and should have been disconnected from the shares—Violent and criminal plan.

CHAPTER VI

The end of the month of December, 1719, was the term of this delusion of three months. A certain number of stockjobbers, better advised than others, or more impatient to enter upon the enjoyment of their riches, combined to dispose of their shares. They took advantage of the rage which led so many to sell their estates—they purchased them, and thus obtained the real for the imaginary. They established themselves in splendid mansions, upon magnificent domains, and made a display of their fortunes of thirty or forty millions. They possessed precious stones and jewels, which were still eagerly offered, and secured solid value in exchange for the semblance of it, which had become so prized by the crowd of dupes. The first effect of this desire to realize was a general increase in the price of everything. An enormous mass of paper being put in the balance with the existing quantity of merchandise and other property, the more paper there was offered against purchasable objects the more rapid the increase became. Cloth, which heretofore brought fifteen to eighteen francs per yard, rose to one hundred and twenty-five francs per yard. In a cook-shop, a *Mississippian*, bidding against a nobleman for a fowl, ran the price up to two hundred francs.

From this instant the shares suffered their first decline, and a heavy uneasiness began to spread abroad. The extent of the fall was not measured by those whom it menaced; but people wondered, doubted, and began to be alarmed. The shares declined to fifteen thousand francs. However, the banknotes were not yet distrusted. The bank was, in fact, entirely distinct from the company, and their fate, up to this time, appeared in no way dependent on each other. The notes had not undergone any fictitious and extraordinary advance. Large amounts had been issued, certainly; but for gold and silver, and upon the deposit of shares. The portion which had been issued upon the deposit of shares partook of the danger of the shares themselves; but no one thought of that, and the banknotes still possessed the entire confidence of the public; only they no longer had the same advantage over specie since the latter had been so much sought by the *realizers*. The notes already began to be presented at the bank for coin, and the vast reserve it had possessed began to diminish perceptibly.

Law did then what governments do so often, and always with ill success: he resorted to forced measures. He declared, in the first place, by decree, that the banknotes should always be worth five percent more than coin.

In consideration of this superiority in value the prohibition which forbade the deposits of gold and silver for bills, at Paris, was taken off, so that notes could be procured at the bank for coin. This permission was simply ridiculous, for no one now wished to exchange specie for paper even at par. But this was not all; the decree declared, that thereafter silver should not be used in payments of over one hundred francs, nor gold in those over three hundred francs. This was forcing the circulation of notes in large payments, and that of specie in small, and was designed to accomplish by violence what could only be expected from the natural success of the bank.

These measures did not bring any more gold and silver to the bank. The necessity of using banknotes in payments of over three hundred francs, gave them a certain forced employment, but did not procure them confidence. Notes were used for large payments, but coin was amassed secretly as a value more real and more assured. The creditors of the state ceased to carry their receipts to the Rue Quincampoix, because they already distrusted the shares; they could not decide to buy real estate, because the price had quadrupled; they suffered the most painful anxiety, and, in their turn, embarrassed the holders of shares who needed the receipts to pay their installments of one-tenth. The catastrophe approached, and nothing could avert it, unless some magic wand could give the company an income of four or five hundred millions a year, which was now only seventy or eighty millions.

Law, having been converted by the Abbé de Tencin, had abjured the Protestant religion, and been appointed Comptroller General of the Finances. He was anxious to revive courage, and, during the 1st of January, 1720, he made his appearance in the Rue Quincampoix, in the full costume of a minister, surrounded by a numerous attendance of noblemen. His presence inspired a remnant of enthusiasm, and revived for a moment all the anticipations. His agents spread the intelligence that new decrees would be issued in favor of the company, that the real value of the shares would be augmented, and that they must rise again immediately, and that the decline was the result of accident.—(Notes 1, 2.)

In fact, Law added new functions to those the company already exercised. He caused the burdens of the receivers of public moneys to be refunded; he gave it the *receipts-general*, and thus gave it the entire administration of the public revenue. He reserved for it the profit on the refinement of gold and silver, and ordered the recoining of certain coins in order to obtain the opportunity for making a new profit. He caused it to be announced that considerable capital was to be devoted by the company to extend the fisheries, and to the erection of new manufactories. He accorded to the subscribers a more extended time of payment of the installments of one-tenth, which reassured many who were embarrassed by the maturity of their obligations. He caused the directors of the company to advertise that it was about to declare a dividend of forty percent upon its nominal capital of three hundred millions, which would be six or seven percent upon its real capital, and which would suppose an income of one hundred and twenty millions a year. As has been shown, this promise was an imposition, for the income could not much exceed eighty millions. At last, as the creditors of the state no longer sought a liquidation of their claims, and complained that while the shares fluctuated the price of real estate had quadrupled, Law issued a new decree, by which all those who did not present their claims on government for liquidation, should suffer a reduction on them of two percent.

To these rigorous measures toward the creditors he added those of persuasion. He published a pamphlet entitled *A Letter to a Creditor*, in which he justified his refunding project. He demonstrated that the system of perpetual annuities was ruinous to the state, and that the abolition of them was a politic measure. He reproached the annuitants for not having subscribed in season, and for not having taken their share of the profits of the rise—a fault, if it was one, imputable to him rather than to them, since he was the author of the proceedings which had prevented the creditors becoming, directly, the shareholders in the company.

These measures produced a transient relief in the market. The shares, which had declined to twelve thousand francs, rose again to fifteen, and it was thought for a moment that they had yielded only to a panic. Besides, every decline is succeeded, in the passion for stock-jobbing, by a reaction, because the decline in the market attracts purchasers who speculate upon a return of the rise. The creditors of the state presented their claims for liquidation, but they hesitated, notwithstanding the hopeful lights which were displayed so brilliantly before them, to invest their money in the Rue Quincampoix, and exchanged their receipts for banknotes, which obliged the bank to raise the issue as high as a billion. In this manner, the amount of the debt, which should have been converted into shares, remained floating in the shape of banknotes.

So the rise was only momentary. The eagerness to sell remained the same; the decline of paper money and the increased price of everything continued in the same proportion. The shares declined to twelve thousand.

The notes also began sensibly to lose their value relative to specie. Their position was, as we have said, different from that of the shares. They represented some commercial funds, some deposits of gold and silver, and much of the national debt recently refunded. All these values were real. There were only the notes representing the shares deposited, which constituted values suspected and tainted by misrepresentation. But, although this was a good reason for discrediting them, the real cause of their decline in value was the increasing disposition to realize. Merchants received the notes, but it was to take them to the bank. These merchants did not wish to realize in Paris all they could; they sent quantities of banknotes away from Paris to convert them into specie, still sufficiently abundant in the treasuries of the provinces.

Law, at the end of his resources, persevered in the employment of forced measures. In order to oppose some obstacle to the eagerness with which people exchanged banknotes for rich ornaments, he prohibited, by decree, the wearing of diamonds pearls and precious stones. To stop the conversion of notes into specie, which the merchants effected in the provinces, he prohibited the transportation of specie between cities where there were branches of the bank. Heretofore he had contented himself with enabling creditors to require payment in banknotes, and afterward by requiring that all payments of more than three hundred francs should be made in notes, but specie still sufficed for ordinary purposes. He settled this difficulty by a decree of the 28th of January, giving a forced currency to banknotes. Law, at last, had recourse to a new alteration of the coin to give a movement to specie and bring it back to the bank. After three days, gold was to be reduced from nine hundred to eight hundred and ten francs to the marc, and silver from sixty to fifty-four. The confiscation of all the old coin was ordered, the recoinage of which had been directed, and which had not been brought to the mint. Domiciliary visits were authorized to discover any infringement of these regulations.

These odious measures did not arrest the continued decline of the shares, nor the progressive, though less rapid, discredit of the banknotes. The shares fell to ten thousand francs. At this time the scene was deplorable. The creditors of the state, their claims paid, their hands full of banknotes, afraid to buy shares, unable to invest in real estate, remained in trembling expectation of the catastrophe which menaced all paper securities. The speculators who had arrived late (toward the end of the rise), having brought to the Rue Quincampoix the sum total of their property, and exchanged their substance for a phantom, were a prey to despair. As to those who had become rich, they rushed into those violent pleasures and excesses which the soul of a gambler craves; they displayed in their newly-acquired mansions, that barbarous, monstrous luxury which signalized the age of Roman corruption; furniture of gold and silver, dazzling jewels, precious odors, fountains of perfumed water, fruits from both continents, monstrous fish, marvellous automatons, half-naked courtesans—this was the display which some of them made at their entertainments. Those who, more cautious, avoided this licentiousness, committed a great wrong toward France, by transferring our specie to foreign countries to ensure certain and unassailable fortunes there. The manners of the people were corrupted by these events. The power, which all classes had, of enriching themselves without that labor which renders man worthy of wealth and temperate in the enjoyment of it, excited among the people an immoderate ambition—an unbridled rage for luxury—and raised up a crowd of vulgar upstarts, strangers to refined pleasures, and abandoned to gross and brutal indulgence.

In such a situation of affairs, it was necessary to take some decided course. It was evident that the decline of the shares would continue without intermission; that soon, a terror seizing upon all minds, the discredit would be as exaggerated as the credit had been, and that the shares would fall temporarily below what they were actually worth. It was necessary to be resigned to this and to submit to the consequences of the fault which had been committed in the conversion of the public debt. It was necessary to let the shares fall, the inordinate advance of which could not be prevented, but to hasten to save the bank, an institution vast, useful, and become, for the moment, sacred. The notes, in fact, had every claim to protection from the shares. The speculators in the shares had undoubtedly been deceived; among them many creditors of the state had been the victims of deplorable illusions; nevertheless they had wished to speculate and had freely taken the chances of fortune. The holders of banknotes, on the contrary, were forced to accept them by the decrees which refunded the public debt, which obliged the payment of all sums over three hundred francs in notes, which, at last, gave a forced currency to them. The notes were a value which the holders had taken without any choice of their own, without seeking the chances of fortune, by force, in obedience to the law. Unless it would subject itself to the charge of actual theft, the law ought to guarantee the value of the notes.

In a word, it was necessary to sacrifice the shares to protect the notes. The means of accomplishing this were very simple, it was to disconnect the fate of the notes from that of the shares. There were a billion francs in banknotes in circulation. A part of this sum had been issued to discount bills of exchange, another part to pay the creditors of the state. These were issued upon a solid foundation, since they represented commercial bills which were soon due, and a part of the public debt. Four hundred and fifty millions had been issued upon shares deposited. These had no foundation. These should have been recalled immediately, by calling in the loans, and thus entirely detaching the notes from the shares. These would have sunk immediately. It was necessary to become callous, to sustain many just reproaches and defy the unjust, and expiate an exaggerated popularity, by suffering an excessive condemnation. The shares would then have risen again, but not beyond the limit where the certain income of the company would have carried them. It had eighty millions that year to divide, it could have one hundred millions the next year. This would give a dividend of five percent, and would be sufficient, at the present rates, to maintain the total capital at two billions, which would give a market price of about three thousand francs a share. At this price, the shares would again have crept by degrees into favor, and the creditors of the state, holders of large sums in banknotes, would have employed them sooner or later in paying the installments. The company would have been saved with the bank, and the system itself would have survived the panic. But what courage was needed to brave the cries of those of the creditors who had been unwittingly led into this fatal course; of that nobility, whose wildest hopes had been nourished; who, in possessing shares, thought their hands filled with gold—who surrounded Law with homage—who regarded him as a benefactor, and called him the *great* Law! How dare he betray their hopes, renounce their adorations, and endure their contempt and fury?

Law conceived a plan, at once violent and criminal, which had the faults which all those have which oppose a necessity, and which risk everything rather than sacrifice anything. He resolved to sustain the banknotes by forced measures, and to join the fate of the shares to that of the notes at the risk of ruining both. Here is his plan in detail.

We have already seen what he had done to compel the employment of notes, and thus sustain their credit. They had been given the currency of coin; they alone could be employed in payments over three hundred francs, and in the transfer of funds from province to province. To these regulations Law added some still more violent. By the decrees of the 23rd and 25th of February, the notes alone could be employed in payments of over one hundred francs. Notwithstanding this extension of the exclusive use of notes, the concealment of coin continued. Law forbade the holding of more than five hundred francs in specie at a time, by any individual, under a penalty of 10,000 francs. Informers were allowed half the fine, which immediately introduced distrust and trouble in families. The prevention of the hoarding of coin did not interdict all outlets for it except the boxes in the treasury. There remained its conversion into furniture and plate. Law limited this fabrication by a series of articles which must be read to enable one to conceive the embarrassments which involve the adoption of forced measures. No work in gold was allowed to weigh more than an ounce. The manufacture of silver plate was still permitted, but the largest dishes could not weigh more than ten marcs, a dozen plates more than thirty marcs, a sugar bowl more than three marcs, candlesticks more than four, etc.

Many articles of furniture and luxury were enumerated, the

manufacture of which in gold or silver was prohibited. After having prevented the hoarding or casting of precious metals, in order to oblige them to be brought to the bank, Law resorted to a proceeding still more censurable: that of another alteration in the value of coin. By the same decrees he raised the marc of silver from sixty to eighty francs, with the purpose of reducing it soon to sixty again. At the moment of the reduction the possessors of coin must necessarily bring it to the bank, to avoid its decline in their hands; but in this case it was the bank which sustained the loss by the reduction, and it attracted coin only by sustaining considerable losses, and by disturbing, besides, all kinds of transactions by this fluctuation in values. The marc being raised from sixty to eighty francs, the coin in France was increased from twelve to sixteen millions.

NOTES TO CHAPTER VI

(1.) A last effort was therefore tried to restore the public confidence in the Mississippi project. For this purpose, a general conscription of all the poor wretches in Paris was made by order of government. Upward of six thousand of the very refuse of the population were impressed, as if in time of war, and were provided with clothes and tools to be embarked for New Orleans, to work in the gold mines alleged to abound there. They were paraded day after day through the streets with their pikes and shovels, and then sent off in small detachments to the outposts to be shipped for America. Two-thirds of them never reached their destination, but dispersed themselves over the country, sold their tools for what they could get, and returned to their old course of life. In less than three weeks afterwards, one-half of them were to be found again in Paris. The manoeuvre, however, caused a trifling advance in Mississippi stock. Many persons of superabundant gullibility believed that operations had begun in earnest in the new Golconda, and that gold and silver ingots would again be found in France.—Mackay's Popular Delusions.

(2.) The vagabonds and refuse of justice having produced nothing but disorder in Mississippi, the company changed its method of recruiting, and, instead of criminals, those alone

whose only crime was poverty were condemned to this exile.—
Cochut.

CHAPTER VII

The bank and the company united—Price of the shares fixed—Measures for regulating the exchange of shares—Frightful depreciation of banknotes—Debtors the only persons benefited—Father betrayed by his son—Speculators dispersed by soldiers—Second *Letter to a Creditor*—Ingratitude of the *Mississippians*—Murder and robbery by a young nobleman—Firmness of the Regent.

CHAPTER VII

The bank and the company were at last united, which was the essential condition of the general plan of Law, but which should not have been effected until the company should have escaped from its troubles by the reduction of its shares to a price proportioned to its actual income. Law issued this decree on the 6th of March, which achieved the grand object of his desires. This decree fixed the price of the shares, for the future, at nine thousand francs. It effected nothing to fix the price in this arbitrary manner; the price must be assured to those who wished to sell. The same decree also ordered the opening of an office at the bank for exchanging shares for notes, or notes for shares, at pleasure, at the price of nine thousand francs a share. By this measure Law thought, or pretended to think, that he had definitely fixed the condition of the shares. The value of notes being assured, according to him, by the different decrees he had issued, that of the shares was assured by the optional conversion of them into notes. The *system* thus tended toward the accomplishment of one of its perfections, which was to offer to the public, at their option, either a profitable investment or a sound currency. This combination offered a profit calculated with great ingenuity. Every share exchanged for notes and deposited in the bank ceased to pay a profit to the depositor, and, of course, was a profit to the company, which received the income on it. In this manner, the dividend earned on the deposited shares increased that on the shares which were held as an investment, not having been exchanged for notes.

This project of a great intellect at bay, contending against an inevitable catastrophe, has been attributed to the ministers of the quadruple alliance by the friends of Law, who have sought to excuse his faults. These ministers, say the apologists of Law, desired to ruin the *system*, and contrived the decree of the 5th of March. The apologists are mistaken. The decree belonged positively to Law; everything proves it—the subtlety of the combination, the care taken to adapt it to the original plan, and the manifest desire to sustain the shares, even at the expense of the notes.

This disastrous project contained the greatest errors at once of principle and of their application. In the first place, the value of the notes was far from being consolidated by the forced measures which had been resorted to; and had it been, it would have been destroyed by the attempt to attach to it the value of the shares. Then it was a grave error to attempt to fix the price of the shares, even if the value had been real and not exaggerated. The shares, representing the capital invested in an enterprise which could have greater or less success, or even no success at all, ought to be uncertain, like the result, and lose or gain according to the chances of success. It should be thus with all investments. The desire to render them more easily disposed of by facilitating the exchange of the scrip was commendable, but the liberation of invested capital, so as to render it convertible at any moment into a fixed sum of money, was to convert it directly into nothing less than money itself; and then interest upon it was "nonsense," for interest is designed to pay for what is not in circulation. It was absurd to wish to fix the price of the shares; moreover, in the existing circumstances, it was criminal. A large number of shares were exchanged for banknotes, and the notes becoming confounded with the imaginary capital of the Rue Quincampoix, must sink with it. At the existing prices, the total number of shares was still worth five or six billions, and must fall inevitably to two billions or fifteen hundred millions. The banknotes must share this bankruptcy, and the involuntary holder of the notes must share the ruin of the *Mississippians*. Without having wished to speculate, without having taken any of the chances, he was despoiled, he was ruined by the law.

Some other provisions, the necessary consequence of the preceding, were contained in the famous decree of the 5th of March, 1720. All the sums lent upon deposits of shares were to be called in, since by the optional conversion a new mode of deposit had been instituted. The loans amounted to four hundred and twenty-five millions. Many of the subscribers not having completed their payments, because they had not the means, or because the creditors no longer brought their *receipts* to the Rue Quincampoix, Law obviated the difficulty by uniting several shares, the first payments on which had been made, to make one share entirely paid in. Four of the ten payments on the great subscription of fifteen hundred shares had been made; that is, two thousand francs of the five due on each. For these two thousand francs and the three still unpaid, the subscriber was entitled to one share, the price of which was then nine thousand. He paid five thousand for what was worth nine thousand; he thus gained four thousand; upon three shares he gained twelve thousand francs. In this manner there was a profit in reducing several shares to one. Three subscriptions, upon which four payments had been made, paid for two shares. These three subscriptions, with four payments on each, made six thousand francs paid in. The subscriber then had, for six thousand francs, two shares at nine thousand francs each, or together, eighteen thousand francs. He gained twelve thousand francs, all as if there had been no confusion.

The company, having been paid four of the ten installments, had received six hundred millions, and was to receive nine hundred more to complete the amount of fifteen hundred millions. By reducing the three hundred shares one-third, which it was the original intention to issue, to obtain the fifteen hundred millions, it left two hundred thousand in the market, and reserved one hundred thousand, which, at nine thousand francs, represented the nine hundred millions remaining to be collected. By this arrangement all the shares issued were wholly paid for; the remainder were simply new shares to be sold. The result of this regulation of the account with the shareholders, was, that a part of the shares were retained by the company, which, according to the first terms of subscription, the subscribers would have been obliged to take. These terms, moreover, had become illusory since the establishment of the office for purchase and sale as every one was at liberty to return his shares to the company. Besides the one hundred thousand shares which the company consented to retain, and which represented the unpaid installments, it took charge of another one hundred thousand belonging to the royal treasury, which had become a subscriber by benevolently taking on its own account the shares of a number of noble families, favorites of the regent. The company agreed to pay nine hundred millions for them, but it was to have three years in which to pay it. This precaution was indispensable, as otherwise it would have been compelled to issue nine hundred millions more of banknotes, and the already overburdened circulation could not possibly have sustained it.

As the creditors, forced to accept payment, would not take the shares in which they no longer had any confidence, and could not buy real estate because of the excessive exaltation in its price, the company was permitted to return to its system of pensions, and to create ten millions of them at two and a half percent. This offered an investment for those who did not know how to make use of their banknotes, and a method for calling in four hundred millions of notes.

These were the measures devised by Law to retard the catastrophe which could not be averted. The office for the purchase and the sale of shares was scarcely opened when the crowd poured into it. Four hundred and twenty-five millions of the billion of notes issued had been recalled by the revocation of the loans on deposits of shares. These had been immediately reissued to pay for the shares presented for exchange. The bank was even compelled to issue another billion to satisfy all the demands, which raised the total issue to two billions.

From this moment the depreciation of banknotes, and the appreciation of everything else, was more rapid than ever. Heretofore the shares being convertible into notes only by sale in the market, the conversion had been little by little, and their value had been exchanged slowly for merchandise, real estate and all kinds of purchasable property. But the power of immediate conversion being given, the whole mass of shares could be realized at once. There were fifteen or sixteen hundred millions realized, as we have just seen. Thus the depreciation made frightful progress. It was no longer the shares which declined, since they could always be converted at will for a fixed sum of banknotes, but the notes themselves depreciated. In February the notes were at a discount of only ten percent, while the shares had fallen one-half. After the decree of the 5th of March the shares no longer declined, but the notes were at forty or fifty percent discount. The shares were still quoted at nine thousand francs: but nine thousand francs in notes were worth only four or five thousand in coin. Violent and vexatious as the measures were to sustain the credit of the notes, they were insufficient to give them a value which they did not possess. No one wished to make use of them; dishonest debtors alone used them to pay their debts. Lessees paid their rent in notes, which operation relieved many of them who were much involved. The nobility, especially, paid all their debts in this way, and thus relieved their estates from the mortgages with which they were encumbered. Law thus accomplished a part of what he had promised them by furnishing them with a means of freeing themselves from debt. But if the notes were good for defrauding old creditors, they were only worth one-half their nominal value for new purchases. Coin was secretly used for daily purchases, and was concealed with care, to avoid the necessity of taking it to the bank. Notwithstanding the prohibition to retain more than five hundred francs in coin, and the inducements offered to informers, many accumulated it clandestinely. It is true that their resistance of the law gave them many pangs. They feared every moment a betrayal by their servants, and even by their nearest relatives. People saw with indignation an unnatural son betray his father. The regent rendered a judgment full of wisdom against the son, and everybody applauded him for it. But the system fell into greater contempt than ever. A frightened few, however, returned their coin to the bank, but the number was small; the greater part buried it in the earth, and the rich *realizers* used every artifice to transfer it to foreign countries. Another portion of coin left France, and although the exportation of specie is not necessarily injurious, it was so at this time, since it left behind only a false paper currency and an imaginary capital.

The Rue Quincampoix was still frequented, but no longer for speculation in shares, but for the exchange of notes for every kind of movable and immovable property. Law prohibited the assembling of crowds in this street, because the price of shares being fixed, they could no longer be the subject of bargains. The crowd persisted, nonetheless, in assembling. Then the archers were sent to disperse the speculators, and these new rigors increased still more the hatred the system and its author inspired.

Under these circumstances Law publislied a second *Letter to a Creditor of the State* upon the whole of his operations. It was dated the 11th of March, 1720. He was right in the principles which he maintained, but he only employed miserable sophisms to justify the exaggerated price to which he had permitted the shares to rise, and at which he had wished to maintain them. All value, he argued, was matter of opinion. Only one thing is necessary to sustain it, i.e. "do not seek to sell." Houses and lands have, indeed, a real value; nevertheless, if everybody wished to sell them at the same time, what would become of it? It was easy to answer this wretched sophism. Lands and houses produce something which establishes the income which they yield, and is a solid foundation of value. On the other hand, it was impossible to establish the supposititious income of the shares, because the business profits could not in any case be proportionate to the extravagant price of the capital. Notwithstanding the certainty of their income, if lands or houses were doubled or tripled in extent or number they would immediately depreciate in proportion. Even if the shares had received such an income, as unfortunately they did not, the immediate creation of such an enormous investment would have caused depreciation. Were there in all France five or six billions of francs to invest in shares bearing interest? Nothing was more false than Law's reasoning. He added to it severe expressions—deserved, but useless—against the *realizers* who precipitated the fall of the *system* by selling their shares.—(Notes 1,2.)

His letter did not allay the irritation. He was called a miserable sophist, and the rich *Mississippians*, whom he accused of ruining the system by *realizing*, inveighed against him with a violence which was, in them, black ingratitude. Some of them exhibited their contempt for paper money by lighting with banknotes the chafing dishes which covered their luxurious tables. A frightful incident augmented still more the general apprehension. In the midst of this delirious cupidity which had seized upon all minds, some profligate young noblemen, who had been unsuccessful in speculation, resolved to steal that which they had not the wit to win. They formed a plot, it was said, to seize the portfolios of the speculators, charging upon them sword in hand as they were assembled in the Rue Quincampoix. A crime committed before the execution of the plot fortunately rendered it impossible. A young roué, the Count de Horn, united with two companions of his debaucheries, and with their aid seized the person of a rich speculator. They carried him to a tavern, where they murdered and then plundered him. They succeeded at first in making their escape, but, pursued by the clamors of the people, they were arrested and confessed their crime. The whole of the nobility surrounded the regent, imploring him to spare the young Count de Horn an infamous punishment. The regent resisted nobly, and answered all that was said on behalf of the family with: "The crime makes the infamy, not the scaffold" Law insisted that the example was indispensable at that time, when everybody had their whole fortune in their portfolios. The Count de Horn expired upon the wheel.

NOTES TO CHAPTER VII

(1.) From the conclusion of this letter we learn that the cares of his station, the pressure of business, or the adulation so lavishly bestowed on him, or perhaps all these causes combined, had begun to affect the minister's brain. "Law's head is so heated that he does not sleep at night, and has terrible fits of frenzy. He gets out of bed almost every night, and runs stark staring mad about the room, making a terrible noise, sometimes singing and dancing, at other times swearing, staring and stamping, quite out of himself. Some nights ago, his wife, who had come into the room upon the noise he made, was forced to ring the bell for people to come to her assistance. The officer of Law's guard was the first that came, and found Law in his shirt, who had set two chairs in the middle of the room, and was dancing round them, quite out of his wits. This scene the officer of the guard told Le Blanc, from whom it came to me by a very sure conveyance."—Hardwicke: *State Papers*.

(2.) "Since Law is comptroller general his head is turned," said the regent. In fact from the very day when the author of the system was disconcerted by the manoeuvre of the *realizers*, it is very difficult to follow his operations—they are like the nervous incoherent movements of a drowning man—Cochut.

CHAPTER VIII

Circulation of gold prohibited—Reduction of the nominal value of shares and banknotes—Great clamor raised—Whole blame of the reduction falls on Law—Regent yields to the clamor—He retains Law in his favor—Law repeals some of the most obnoxious regulations—Measures to abolish the *System*—Difficulties in carrying them out.

CHAPTER VIII

Law, adding measures to measures, at prohibited the circulation of gold, because this metal was, by its convenience, a rival of banknotes infinitely more dangerous than silver. He then announced an approaching reduction in the value of coin, which he had raised by a decree in February, only to reduce it again in a short time. The marc in silver, raised from sixty to eighty francs, was reduced to seventy on the 1st of April, and sixty-five on the 1st of May. But this measure was utterly insufficient to bring it to the bank.

The situation grew worse every day; the issue of notes to pay for the shares presented at the bank had risen to two billions, six hundred and ninety-six millions; their depreciation increased, and creditors of every description being paid in paper which was at a discount of sixty percent, complained bitterly of the theft authorized by law.

In this juncture there remained but one step to be taken. As the necessary sacrifice had not been made in the first place, and the shares abandoned to their fate in order to protect the notes, both must now be sacrificed, shares and notes together, in order to finish this wicked fiction. The falsehood of this nominal value, which obliged men to receive at par what was depreciated thirty or forty percent, could not be prolonged. The immediate reduction of the nominal value of the shares and banknotes was the only resource. Sacrifices cannot be too hastily made when they are inevitable.

M. d'Argenson, although dismissed from the treasury, still remained keeper of the seals; he had risen in the esteem of the regent, as Law had declined, and he advised the reduction of the nominal value of the shares and notes as an urgent necessity. Law, who saw in this reduction an avowal of the fiction in the legal values, and a blow which must hasten the fall of the *system*, opposed it with his whole strength. Nevertheless, M. d'Argenson prevailed. On the 21st of May, 1720, a decree, which remains famous in the history of the *system*, advertized the progressive reduction in the value of shares and notes. This reduction was to begin on the very day of the publication of the decree, and to continue from month to month until the 1st of December. At this last term the shares were to be estimated at five thousand francs, and a banknote of ten thousand francs at five thousand—one of a thousand at five hundred, etc. The notes were thus reduced fifty percent, and the shares only four-ninths percent. Law, although opposed to the decree, consented to promulgate it.—(Note 1.)

Scarcely was it published when a fearful clamor was raised on all sides. The reduction was called a bankruptcy; the government was reproached with being the first to throw discredit upon the values which it had created, with having robbed its own creditors, a number of whom had just been paid in banknotes, even as late as the preceding day; in a word, with assailing the fortunes of all the citizens. The crowd wished to sack Law's hotel, and to tear him in pieces. Nothing that could have happened would have produced a greater clamor; but in times like those it was not only necessary not to fear these clamors—it was even a duty to defy them.—(Notes 2, 3.)

The reply to the complaints would have soon been evident to the intelligence of everybody. Without doubt the creditors of the state, and some private individuals, who had been paid in banknotes, were half ruined by the reduction, but this was not the fault of the decree of the 21st of May—the real reduction was long before this; the decree only stated a loss already experienced and the notes were worth still less than the decree declared. Because a number of creditors had been ruined by the falsity of nominal values, was it a reason to continue the fiction that it might extend the ruin? On the contrary, it was necessary to put an end to it, to save others from becoming victims. The official declaration of the fact, although it was known before, must produce a shock and hasten the discredit, but it was of little importance that it was hastened, since it was inevitable.

The public thought Law the author of this measure, advised exclusively by M. d'Argenson, and he became the sole object of hatred. The parliament, making common cause with the public, thought it a good opportunity to take up arms. It did not perceive, in its blind hatred of the system, that it was going to render a service to its author, and that to declare itself against the reduction of the banknotes was to maintain that the values created by Law had a solid foundation. It assembled on the 27th of May to demand a revocation of the decree of the 21st. At the very moment when it was deliberating, the regent sent one of his officers to prohibit all discussion, announcing the revocation of the decree.

The regent had the weakness to yield to the public clamor. Had the decree been bad, its revocation would have been worse. To declare that the shares and notes were still worth what they purported to be, availed nothing; for no one believed it, and their credit was not restored by it. A legal falsehood was reaffirmed, and, without rendering any service to those who were already ruined, the ruin of those who were obliged to receive the notes at their nominal value was ensured. The decree of the 21st of May, wise if it had been sustained, became disastrous as soon as it was revoked. Its only effect was to hasten the general discredit, without the essential advantage of reestablishing a real, legal value.

The regent feigned, in public, to attribute all the evils of the situation to Law, and to remove him from the general control; but he received him in private, and offered him secret consolation for his seeming severity. The first irritation of the holders being past, he welcomed him publicly again; he even received him in his box at the opera, and gave him a guard to protect his house from the attacks of the mob. The Cardinal Dubois was indebted to the *system* for considerable benefits, and he united with Law in an effort to ruin M. d'Argenson, the author of the decree of the 21st of May. The regent, who, notwithstanding his superiority of intellect and his military courage, lacked resolution, suffered himself to be persuaded, took the seals from M. d'Argenson, and gave them to M. d'Aguesseau.

Law and the Chevalier de Conflans hastened to Fréne in search of M. d'Aguesseau, who had the weakness to suffer himself to be brought back by the author of his first disgrace. Having returned to Paris, he suffered in the public estimation, and the affairs of the company underwent no improvement.

We have seen by what a succession of faults the *system* had been compromised. This conversion of the public debt into shares having been managed imprudently, the shares had been carried to a price absurdly exaggerated. The fault having been committed, the shares should have been suffered to fall, and have been entirely disconnected with the notes, in order to save the bank at least, an institution of immense utility, if not to save the Indian Company, the success of which was of much less importance. Instead of this, there was an effort to save the shares by means of the notes, which effort compromised both. After this, it was necessary to keep pace with the discredit, and to declare it as fast as it progressed, so that no one should be compelled to accept a false value. But by declaring it, and then revoking the declaration, everything was at once lost. The public, after this, wished to have nothing to do either with shares or notes. There was nothing left but to withdraw both as promptly as possible. A prudent demolition was all that remained to be accomplished.

Law still presided over financial operations without appearing to control them. He was obliged, on the 1st of June, to make a first atonement to the public, by revoking the prohibition to retain more than five hundred francs of coin. This was the most vexatious measure of the *system*, and the revocation of it was the most urgent.

Of the six hundred thousand shares there had been three hundred thousand returned to the bank. The royal treasury had returned one hundred thousand, which made four hundred thousand which the public no longer wanted. In exchange for them there were two billions six hundred and ninety-six millions four hundred thousand banknotes in circulation. These rejected shares must be abolished, and an investment in government securities offered for this mass of notes; that is to say, a return must be made to the old form of the public debt, after frightful disasters and thousands of ruined fortunes. On the 3rd of June the four hundred thousand shares in the bank were annulled. The government voluntarily sacrificed the one hundred thousand which it had deposited, and released the company from its debt of nine hundred millions. This left two hundred thousand shares in circulation, one-third of the whole amount. But, in return, the forty-eight millions, which were assigned to the company upon the collection of the revenue, were retracted to serve for the creation of the new pensions. Of its eighty millions of income, the company thus lost forty-eight, and retained only thirty-two. The two hundred thousand shares remaining in circulation gained by the annulment of the four hundred thousand, since their number was reduced two-thirds, while they did not lose two-thirds of their income. In consideration of this, an assessment of three thousand francs a share was asked, which might be paid either in shares or notes. If in shares, it would take one in three—that is, three shares would be exchanged for two. It seems from this, that the shares were valued at six thousand francs, as one sufficed to pay two assessments of three thousand francs. The assessment was not compulsory. The company promised a dividend of two hundred francs upon the shares not paying the assessments, and three hundred and sixty upon the others. It calculated upon an income of forty millions at least, and seventy-two at most—an entirely exaggerated expectation; for, by the withdrawal of the forty-eight millions on the collection of the revenue, the income was reduced to thirty-two millions. However, by this demand for an assessment, six hundred millions of notes might be recalled, or the two hundred thousand remaining shares might be reduced one-third.

By decrees of the 10th and 20th of June, the forty-eight millions allowed the company on the collection of the revenue was again appropriated by the government, for the service of the new pensions, etc., which it proposed to create. By the decrees of the 24th of February and the 5th of March, a subscription had been opened for ten millions perpetual annuities upon the company and four millions of life annuities. Upon these there had been subscribed one million of perpetual annuities and four millions of life annuities, which made five millions to deduct from the forty-eight millions reassigned to the government. Forty-three millions remained to be employed in the creation of new annuities. There were twenty-five millions constituted upon a capital of a billion, which was two and one-half percent. There remained eighteen millions to be disposed of according to circumstances.

As this investment would not suit those holders of notes who were engaged in commerce, accounts current were opened with them at the bank on the 13th of July, with the double design of offering them a suitable employment for their notes, and to keep up the exercise of the functions of the bank. The money for these current accounts was to be furnished in notes, and not to exceed six hundred millions. For this capital the bank undertook to open accounts with businessmen, and to make their payments through the bank. The billion of annuities and the six hundred millions in current accounts would reduce the two billions six hundred and ninety-six millions of notes which burdened the circulation to about one billion. The assessment demanded on the shares, and the eighteen millions remaining upon the product of the revenue, were so much means of extinguishing this billion.

Such were the measures taken to abolish the *system*. But the recall of the banknotes was not effected without difficulty. The annuities of two and a half percent were not subscribed for with enthusiasm, because the creditors of the state were not contented to receive that interest in the place of the four percent which they received formerly. Yet the two and a half percent was sufficient; for, according to the then value of the notes, it amounted to five percent. But the importunate creditors, who had received the notes at their full value, did not reason in this manner, and believed that two and a half percent, was all they received, and really that was all they obtained on their original capital. So they could not readily bring themselves to make this grievous sacrifice by subscribing for the newly created annuities. The traders were not more eager to open their current accounts, because the bank was distrusted, and the established value of money was of little use in commercial transactions. Of the six hundred millions only two were subscribed. The example which

Law set, by subscribing five millions for annuities and accounts current, had no influence. Neither would the holders of the two hundred thousand shares pay the requested assessments, because they had no confidence either in the dividend of three hundred and sixty francs, or even in that of two hundred.

Although the price of the shares was fixed at six thousand francs for the assessment, they were worth much less for purposes of traffic. Their decline was more rapid than that of the notes, and they had fallen to five thousand francs. Five thousand francs in banknotes were worth scarcely twenty-five hundred in coin. So the share which was worth eighteen thousand francs in November and December, 1719, was worth only twenty-five hundred in June, 1720, eight months after. Although the bank was exempted from paying, at sight, notes of above one hundred francs, by the law which prohibited the payment in coin of sums above that amount, it was, nevertheless, constrained to pay those below that sum. To conceal the exhaustion of its treasury it paid very slowly, and often in the smallest coin. Its offices were opened late and closed early, so that the bills of one hundred francs, and less, were far from being equivalent to coin, on account of the difficulty of converting them.

Banknotes and Denominations in Circulation

There were in notes of	10,000	francs	1,184,000,000
"	1,000	"	1,223,200,000
"	100	"	299,200,000
"	10	"	40,000,000
Making a total of			2,696,400,000

The bank being required to pay only notes of one hundred francs and ten francs, was obliged to find coin only for the
sum (in notes of 100 francs) of 299,200,000
And the sum (in notes of 10 francs) of 40,000,000

Total 339,200,000

This explains the decline in the notes which were not convertible, and the reason why the bank was able, sometimes, to pay on demand.

NOTES TO CHAPTER VIII

(1.) There is abundance of authority that Law was opposed to the fatal edict (21st of May) which changed the relations of coin to the banknotes.—Wood.

(2.) Such were the consequences of the fatal edict of the 21st of May, a piece of folly hardly to be equalled in the annals of any nation, and not easily to be accounted for on any other supposition than as a contrivance of the French ministry to free themselves from a formidable rival, to accomplish which object they did not hesitate to bring the kingdom to the brink of destruction. But it is by no means so easy to account for the regent's giving his consent to a decree that, besides being a breach of public faith, was an experiment full of dangers, by which neither himself nor any other could possibly be benefited. Had no such step been taken, and his highness allowed the system to go on in the way supposed to have been at first intended, it is not unreasonable to imagine that, infatuated as the people were to acquire shares of the India Company, the sums paid to the national creditors would have been retired with the sale of less that 200,000, consequently, the public would then have had about 400,000 shares in their hands. The company could, in this case, easily have made good their engagement to pay a dividend of 200 livres on each of these shares, as we have seen that, on a very moderate computation, they enjoyed an annual revenue of about eighty millions, administered by themselves, and capable of great increase. By destroying the notes retired, none would have remained in circulation except such as had been issued for value by the bank, which could thus have answered all demands made upon it. The company, being thereby relieved from every apprehension of suffering by a run upon them, would have had leisure to direct their attention to the improvement, by all possible means, of the home revenue, the culture of the colonies, and the extension of their commerce. In this case, what might not have been expected from the exertions of a body of men, possessed of almost unlimited credit, whose funds were immense, who had in their hands the whole foreign trade and possessions, and all the public revenues of the kingdom, and who, moreover, enjoyed the declared protection of government, and the implicit confidence of the people? The opinion that the system was a monstrous and impracticable monopoly appears to have been taken up without sufficient grounds. All preceding attempts to establish a flourishing trade to the Indies had failed of success, from deficiency of funds in the parties concerned, so that it was far from being an improper step to endeavor to settle the commerce to these places on a solid and extensive basis, the more especially as the exclusive privilege of trading thereto was granted to the company only for a limited period. With regard to taking the great farms out of the hands of the farmers-general, it is apprehended that the propriety of that transfer will not be disputed, when the enormous profits made by those extravagant and luxurious financiers, and their unwarrantable exactions, are considered; while, on the other hand, the superior advantages of assuming these favors into the hands of a company, in which no person that could command a moderate sum was excluded from holding a share, is evident. By consolidating into one channel every branch of the public revenue, all unnecessary charges of collection and mismanagement were avoided and consequently the taxes must be levied and their amounts remitted at the cheapest rate possible. At least it must be acknowledged that the idea was truly great; and Mr. Law's being able to carry matters to the length he did, will appear astonishing indeed when we consider what reception would in this country await a similar attempt to unite the public revenues, the mint, the banks, the East India and other privileged companies, into the hands of one great association. The very low price at which the shares of the India Company were originally fixed must however be allowed to have been a capital error, though, perhaps, in some measure necessary to raise the *billets d'etat* from the discredit into which they had fallen.—Wood.

(3.) Among the caricatures that were abundantly published, and that showed as plainly as graver matters that the nation had awakened to a sense of its folly; was one, a facsimile of which is preserved in the *Mémoires de la Régence*. It was thus described by its author: The Goddess of Shares in her triumphal car, driven by the Goddess of Folly. Those who are drawing the car are impersonations of the Mississippi, with his wooden leg, the South Sea, the bank of England, the Company of the West of Senegal, and of various assurances. Lest the car should not roll fast enough, the agents of these companies, known by their long fox-tails and their cunning looks, turn round the spokes of the wheels, upon which are marked the names of the several stocks and their value, sometimes high and low according to the turns of the wheel. Upon the ground are the merchandise, daybooks and ledgers of legitimate commerce, crushed under the chariot of Folly. Behind is an immense crowd of persons of all ages, sexes, and conditions, clamoring after Fortune, and fighting with each other to get a portion of the shares which she distributed so bountifully among them. In the clouds sits a demon, blowing bubbles of soap, which are also the objects of the admiration and cupidity of the crowd, who jump upon one another's backs to reach them ere they burst. Right in the pathway of the car, and blocking up the passage, stands a large building, with three doors, through one of which it must pass if it proceeds further, and, all the crowd along with it. Over the first door are the words, "*Hôpital des Foux*" over the second, "*Hôpitaldes Malades*" and over the third, "*Hôpitaldes Gueux*." Another caricature represented Law sitting in a large caldron, boiling over the flames of popular madness, surrounded by an impetuous multitude, who were pouring all their gold and silver into it, and receiving gladly in exchange the bits of paper which he distributed among them by handfuls.—Mackay's *Popular Delusions*.

CHAPTER IX

"Spoils of the *Mississippians*"—Further efforts to bring in the notes—Men suffocated in the crowd at the bank—Mob pursue Law—He seeks protection at the palace of the Regent—Bank closed—Tampering with the currency—Severities towards the *Mississippians*—Final abolition of the System—Law quits France—Confiscation of his property.

CHAPTER IX

The stockjobbers still sought to assemble for buying and selling. Driven from the Rue Quincampoix, they formed groups in the Place Vendôme. The existence of an open office at the bank, for the exchange of shares and notes, could no longer be an objection to their assembling, so they were authorized to assemble. They raised tents in the Place Vendôme on account of the excessive heat in July. Under these tents various bargains were made—shares were sold for notes; notes for specie or merchandise, consisting of jewelry, precious stones, ornaments, furniture, and even horses and carriages which had belonged to ruined speculators. It was a fair where were sold the spoils of the *Mississippians*. The public called it *Mississippi overthrown*.

Law conceived a new means of insuring the return of notes, which had been heretofore neglected.

The company had certain privileges for nine years only, and others for fifty. Law prepared a decree which secured these privileges to it in perpetuity, on the condition that six hundred millions of notes should be called in. It was a more certain method than the assessments on the bank accounts. The decree was presented to parliament on the 17th of July.

The same day there occurred a very important incident.

We have just said that the bank was not obliged to pay notes of over one hundred francs. It paid them slowly, and employed all imaginable artifices to avoid the payment of them. Nevertheless, its coffers were almost exhausted, and it was necessary to authorize it to confine its disbursements to the payment of notes of ten francs only. The people rushed to the bank in crowds, to *realize* their notes of ten francs, fearing that these would soon share the fate of those of one hundred. The pressure was so great that three persons suffocated. The indignant mob, ready for any excess, already menaced the house of Law. He fled to the Palais Royal to seek an asylum near the regent. The mob followed him, carrying the bodies of the three who had been suffocated. The carriage which had just conveyed him was broken to pieces, and it was feared that even the residence of the regent would not be respected.

The gates of the court of the Palais Royal had been closed; the Duke of Orleans, with great presence of mind, ordered them to be opened. The crowd rushed into the court and suddenly stopped upon the steps of the palace. Leblanc, the chief of police, advanced to those who bore the corpses, and said, "My friends, go place these bodies in the Morgue, and then return to demand your payment." These words calmed the tumult; the bodies were carried away and the sedition was quelled.

In the midst of these popular tumults, parliament assembled to act upon the edict which accorded to the company its privileges in perpetuity.

The session was a stormy one, and from time to time members would ask, in defiance of all decency, if Law had not yet been killed by the people? They were vexed to learn that he had found safety with the regent, and took the opportunity to refuse to enregister the edict.

In order to prevent the recurrence of these popular outbreaks, notice was given that the bank would be closed for a few days, but, to keep the people quiet, money-changers were distributed in the principal public places to receive a portion of the notes of ten francs. Law remained concealed at the Palais Royal to avoid the public sentiment, and the parliament was exiled to Pontoise.

After this, measures succeeded each other rapidly, designed to call in the paper in circulation and hasten the complete abolition of the *system*. Having been unable to reduce the nominal value of notes and shares one-half, that of coin was doubled. The marc of gold, raised to eighteen hundred francs, and that of silver to one hundred and twenty, were both to be reduced, from month to month, to their first prices, of nine hundred and of sixty. This was done to induce a return of silver into circulation. The measure was ruinous to creditors, who, having made their bargains when the marc of silver was sixty francs, were paid when it was one hundred and twenty.

Decrees were then published with the design of withdrawing the banknotes as fast as possible. As the public were not disposed to subscribe for the annuities, shares were again resorted to, and fifty thousand created in order to withdraw the six hundred millions with which the company had intended to pay for the perpetuity of their privileges. The assessments were made compulsory, under penalty of annulment of the shares. Eight millions, of two percent, annuities were created to furnish the creditors in the provinces an opportunity to use their securities. At last, to put an end to the circulation of the notes, it was decided that the notes of ten thousand francs and those of one thousand, should become preferred shares, with a fixed income of two percent. They were thus condemned to take the form of shares, without even having the chance of increasing their dividend, if the operations of the company should be fortunate.

This decree, which announced the approaching end of the *system*, accelerated still more the decline of the notes of ten thousand and of one thousand francs. The bank, in order to conform to the progressive depreciation, had been obliged to reduce the two hundred millions, furnished for opening the accounts current, to fifty millions. The shares now sold for only two thousand francs in bills, which represented scarcely two hundred in silver, so that the shares which had sold for eighteen thousand francs, in November, 1719, were worth only two hundred in October, 1720.

The market for stocks, which had been transferred from the Place Vendôme to the Hôtel de Soissons, was again closed. Sixty brokers were appointed to act as agents for sales and purchases, and all assembling of speculators in public places was prohibited.

Severities against the rich *Mississippians* were commenced in this same month of October. For a long time, it had been suspected that the government, following an ancient usage, would deprive them, by means of *visas* and *chambres ardentes*, of what they had acquired by stock-jobbing. A list was made of those known to have speculated in shares. A special commission arbitrarily placed on this list the names of those whom public opinion designated as having enriched themselves by speculation in paper. They were ordered to deposit a certain number of shares at the offices of the company, and to purchase the required number, if they had sold their own. The *realizers* were thus brought back by force to the company which they had deserted. Eight days were given to speculators of good faith to make, voluntarily, the prescribed deposit. To prevent flight from the country, it was prohibited, under pain of death, to travel without a passport.

These measures increased still more the decline of the shares. All those whose names were not upon the list of rich speculators, and who could not tell what would become of the shares not yet deposited, hastened to dispose of all they retained.

The *system* wholly disappeared in November, 1720, one

year after its greatest credit. All the notes were converted into annuities or preferred shares, and all the shares were deposited with the company. Then a general *visa* was ordered, consisting of an examination of the whole mass of shares, with the purpose of annulling the greater portion of those which belonged to the enriched stockjobbers.—(Note 1.)

Law, foreseeing the renewed rage which the *visa* would excite, determined to leave France. The hatred against him had been so violent since the scene of the 17th of July, that he had not dared to quit the Palais Royal. The following fact will give an idea of the fury excited against him: A hackman, having a quarrel with the coachman of a private carriage, cried out, "There is Law's carriage." The crowd rushed upon the carriage, and nearly tore in pieces the coachman and his master before it could be undeceived.—(Notes 2, 3, 4.)

Law demanded passports of the Duke of Orleans, who granted them immediately. The Duke of Bourbon, made rich by the system, felt under obligations to Law, and offered money and the carriage of Madame de Prie, his mistress. Law refused the money and accepted the carriage. He repaired to Brussels, taking with him only eight hundred louis.—(Notes 8, 9.)

Scarcely was he gone when his property, consisting of lands and shares, was sequestrated.

Law had been imprudent, culpable, even, in his management of the *system*, but he thought more of carrying out his views than of making a fortune. While the rich *Mississippians* had acquired fortunes of forty or fifty millions, he, possessor of all the treasure of the system, had made scarcely ten, had invested them in France and had sent nothing abroad. Able to draw large sums in coin at the bank, he did not even think to procure money for his journey, and owed to accident the eight hundred louis which served to pay his travelling expenses. His property was sequestrated on the pretext of regulating his personal accounts with the company, of which, however, he was the creditor.—(Notes 5, 6, 7.)

The brothers Paris were charged with the execution of the *visa*. It extended to two billions two hundred and twenty-two millions of the paper of the *system* still remaining, and consisted of shares, or notes converted into preferred shares. The title by which these were held, by those who had deposited them, was investigated, and those belonging to lately enriched holders Were annulled, which reduced the total amount of paper to five hundred millions. The public debt was thus changed—partly into annuities and partly into shares. The capital was nearly the same as before the *system*, but the interest was very much diminished. There was but little more than thirty-seven millions to pay, instead of eighty millions; but a very large number of creditors had been completely ruined and the public credit was as low as in 1716. The bank was abolished—the company, deprived of all its privileges except that of foreign commerce, continued to exist under the name of the Indian Company, and was all that remained of the vast machine which Law had contrived.

NOTES TO CHAPTER IX

Law's Perilous Situation

(1.) The *visa* appointed to settle this complicated and difficult liquidation consisted of fifteen boards, composed of Masters of Bequests and Counsellors of the Great Council, who employed under them no less than 800 clerks; and, in order to assist the commissioners in their operations, copies of all contracts for the transfer of property entered into before notaries, between 1st July, 1719, and 31st December, 1720, were directed to be made out. The effects, carried to the *visa* by 511,009 individuals, amounted, as stated by the proprietors, to 2,222,597,491 livres in contracts for annuities on lives, perpetual annuities, etc. And this sum the commissioners reduced to 1,676,501,831 livres, the interest of which may be computed at forty-eight millions a year, partly consisting in life annuities, and therefore continually diminishing. The shares of the India Company were in like manner reduced from 125,024, with a dividend of 360 livres per annum each, to only 55,316 (afterward increased to 56,000), each having a dividend of 100 livres the first year, and 150 livres every subsequent year, exclusive of their proportion of the profits of the trade. Thus, in consequence of these arbitrary proceedings, the annual interest payable by the king was diminished to about fifty-six millions of livres, by which his majesty was a gainer of upwards of forty millions a year, and many of the public creditors were reduced to the utmost misery and distress.—Wood.

(2.) In the midst of these disordered movements, the situation of Law had become very perilous. The Count de Braglie, who affected great frankness, had dared to say at the table of the regent, and looking the director in the face, that he would die on the gallows. Bets were made on the London Exchange that he would be hung in September; Law, himself, brave as he was, was frightened and did not conceal it. He feared that some intrigue of the court, or some riot in the street, would put a tragic end to his existence. "I am," said he, "like the chicken with golden eggs, who was worth no more, dead, than a common fowl."—Cochut.

(3.) The parliament was sitting at the time of this uproar, and the President took upon himself to go out and see what was the matter. On his return, he informed the councillors that Law's carriage had been broken by the mob. All the members rose simultaneously, and expressed their joy by a loud shout, while one man, more zealous in his hatred than the rest, exclaimed, "And Law himself, is he torn to pieces?"—Mackay's *Popular Delusions*.

(4.) Every epithet that popular hatred could suggest was showered upon the regent and the unhappy Law. Coin, to any amount above five hundred livres, was an illegal tender, and nobody would take paper if he could help it. No one knew today what his notes would be worth tomorrow. "Never," says Duclos, in his *Secret Memoirs of the Regency*, "was seen a more capricious government—never was a more frantic tyranny exercised by hands less firm. It is inconceivable to those who were witnesses of the horrors of those times, and who look back upon them now as on a dream, that a sudden revolution did not break out—that Law and the regent did not perish by a tragical death. They were both held in horror, but the people confined themselves to complaints; a sombre and timid despair, a stupid consternation, had seized upon all, and men's minds were too vile even to be capable of a courageous crime." There was still one more trial left: on the 12th of November, he having appeared at the bank, they called him knave and thief to his face. He left, his head high and his look disdainful, and only thought to prepare for departure.—Cochut.

(5.) At his last interview with the Duc d'Orleans, it is reported that Mr. Law said, "My Lord, I acknowledge that I have committed great faults; I did so because I am but a man, and all men are liable to err; but I declare to your royal highness that none of them proceeded from knavery, and that nothing of that kind will be found in the whole course of my conduct."

The absurdity of this last accusation is evident; and with respect to the charge of knavery, a very strong proof of the uprightness of his intentions arises from the circumstance of vesting his whole acquisitions in landed property in France, not remitting any part thereof to foreign countries, which could have been done with the utmost facility, and obliging his immediate connections, particularly his brother William, and his confidential secretary, Robert Neilson, to follow the same honorable line of conduct. The amount of Mr. Law's fortune at the conclusion of the system, will afford another refutation of the charge. The following enumeration of his purchases in France (see overleaf) being stated on the authority of his nephew, M. Law de Lauriston:

Enumeration of the Purchases of John Law

	Livres
Le Marquisat d'Effiat (en Auvergne)	800,000
La Terre de la Riviere	900,000
Le Marquisat de Toucy	160,000
La Terre de la Marche	120,000
La Terre de Roissy	650,000
La Terre d'Orcher	400,000
Terre et Bois de Brean	160,000
Marquisats de Charleville et Bacqueville	330,000
La Terre de Berville	200,000
La Terre de Fontaine Rome	130,000
La Terre de Serville	110,000
La Terre d'Yville	200,000
La Terre de Gerponville	220,000
La Terre de Tancarville (en Normandie)	320,000
La Terre de Guermande	160,000
Hotel Mazarin, et Emplacemens Rue Vivienne	1,200,000
Emplacemens Rue de Varenne	110,000
Emplacemens de la Place Louis le Grand	250,000
Partie du fief de la Grange Batelière	150,000
Marais ou Chantiers du Fauxbourg St. Honore	160,000
Maisons, surtout dans Paris	700,000
Les Domains de Bourget	90,000
Quelques petites terres, comme Valançay, St. Suplice, etc.	350,000
	7,870,000

(6.) Besides the above, it is said that he acquired Lislebonne from the Marchioness de Beuveron, at the price of 500,000 livres, and also Little Rambouillet at 180,000 livres; made offer of 1,700,000 livres to the Duke de Sully for the Marquisate of Rosny, purchased the valuable library of the Abbé Bignon at the price of 180,000 livres, and bought, for 150,000 livres, the Secrétaire du Roi, for the sake of the privileges of nobility attached to that office. But the making of these purchases was reckoned a piece of policy necessary for the support of his own credit, and of that of the India Company; and so strict a connection subsisted between these, that it was remarked on disposing of part of his landed property, people began to speak in very dubious terms of his circumstances, and the price of shares suffered a depression.—Wood.

(7.) It would seem that Mr. Law originally possessed 10,500 shares of the India Company. Of these he voluntarily gave up 2,000 to the company in October, 1720; 3,000 were deposited in security of a debt of £96,000 sterling, due from him to the Earl of Londonderry, Governor Harrison, and other gentlemen; and 500 were assigned for the liquidation of an unjust claim against him, to be hereafter noticed. The deficiency of eight shares of the remaining 5,000, appears to have been owing to the following circumstance: Soon after his elevation to the office of Comptroller-General he made his appearance in the Rue Quincampoix; during the confusion occasioned by the crowd pressing to see him, and crying out *Vive le Roi et Monsieur Law*, a lady had her pocket picked of near 100,000 livres in notes. On being informed thereof, Mr. Law generously presented her with shares to the amount of what she had lost.—Wood.

(8.) Mr. Law arrived at Brussels in the morning of the 22nd December, 1720, passing under the name of M. Du Jardin; but as soon as it was known who he really was, General Wrangle the governor, the Marquis de Pancalliers and several of the principal persons in that city went to pay their respects to him. He waited on the Marquis de Prie the same afternoon at five o'clock, and afterwards accompanied Madame de Pancalliers to the theatre where a vast concourse of people were assembled to behold so extraordinary a character. Next day, the 23rd, the Marquis de Prie, returning Mr. Law's visit in great state, brought him home in his coach to a most sumptuous entertainment, at which were present several persons of the highest quality. That evening Mr. Law went again to the play, and, after it was over, supped with the Marquis d'Esquiblache. On the 24th he dined a second time with the Marquis de Prie, to whom, having notified his intention of leaving Brussels the same evening, that nobleman ordered passports to be got ready; and Mr. Law accordingly set out at nine at night, accompanied by his son.

He came to Venice early in January, 1721, still passing under the name of Mr. Du Jardin, and continued in that city two months, partaking of all the pleasures the Carnival afforded, and living on terms of intimacy with the imperial and French Ambassadors. The famous Cardinal Alberoni, the Spanish minister, coming there in February, had an interview with Mr. Law; and it was reported that the Chevalier de St. George also arrived *incognito* and had a conference with these ministers, in the Capuchin monastery. Whether this last particular was true or not, cannot now be certainly known; only it seems that at this period the chevalier was not seen publicly at Rome for several days, and when he appeared again he looked so well, that little credit was given to the report that had been circulated of his indisposition. In the meantime, the most extraordinary stories were told of Mr. Law, tending to impress people with an idea of his being possessed of immense wealth. It was said that 160,000 pistoles had been lodged on his account in the bank of the Holy Ghost at Rome by some persons unknown; that he had offered a vast sum to be admitted into the order of Venetian nobility; and that his son was to be married to a daughter of the Duc de

Cesarini, who had a fortune of 100,000 crowns; and that he had drawn bills of exchange to the amount of 250,000 pistoles. While such reports were spread, Mr. Law found himself under the necessity, in order to secure himself against the claims of pretended creditors, of having his name enrolled in the list of Roman citizens, it being one of the privileges of that body to be exempted from arrest and prosecution from debt, at the suit of any other than a fellow burgher. Having taken this necessary precaution, he left Venice on the 15th of March, for Ferrara, on his way to Rome, but receiving intelligence that some of his creditors had assigned their debts to a Roman citizen, who had concerted measures to have him arrested immediately on his arrival, he judged it advisable to return to Venice. After some stay there he travelled through Bohemia and Germany to Hanover, where he had the honor of an audience of Prince Frederick, and then proceeded to Copenhagen. During his residence at this place, having received an invitation from the British Ministry to return to his native country, he embarked onboard the Baltic squadron, commanded by Sir John Norris, being accommodated in that admiral's own ship. Landing at the Nore, 20th of October, 1721, he proceeded to London, was presented to King George I, by Sir John, and took a house in Conduit Street, where he was daily visited by numbers of persons of the first quality and distinction.

The favorable manner in which Mr. Law was received, occasioned no small umbrage to the anti-ministerial party, and was judged of sufficient importance to occupy the attention of parliament. For when the House of Lords met on the 26th of October, Earl Coningsby represented to that august assembly how dangerous it might he on several accounts to entertain and countenance such a man as Mr. Law, and desired that a day might be appointed for taking this matter into consideration. Their lordships having appointed the 9th November for the discussion of this business, Earl Coningsby on that day resumed his argument, saying that for his part he could not but entertain great jealousy of a person who had done so much mischief in a neighboring kingdom, and who, being so immensely rich as he was reported to be, might do a great deal more hurt here by tampering with, many who were grown desperate by being involved in the calamity occasioned by the fatal imitation of his pernicious projects; that this person was the more dangerous, in that he had renounced not only his natural affection to his country and his allegiance to his lawful sovereign, by being naturalized in France, and openly countenancing the Pretender's friends; but, which was worst of all, and weighed most with him, that he had also renounced his God by turning Roman Catholic; concluding, that their lordships ought to inquire whether Sir John Norris had orders to bring him over. To this last part of the Earl's speech, Lord Carteret answered in substance, that Mr. Law had, many years ago, the misfortune to kill a gentleman in a duel, but that, having received the benefit of the king's clemency, and the appeal lodged by the relatives of the deceased being taken off, he was come over to plead his majesty's gracious pardon; that there was no law to keep an Englishman out of his own country; and as Mr. Law was a subject of Great Britain, it was not even in the king's power to hinder him from coming home if he thought fit. To this Lord Trevor replied, that Mr. Law was indeed a subject of Great Britain, and, therefore, as such, had an undoubted right to come into the kingdom; but that the circumstance of a person of his character being brought on board of an English Admiral, and at this juncture, might deserve the consideration of the House. Earl Cowper spoke much to the same effect; but the matter was suffered to drop; and Mr. Law, on the 28th of November following, pleaded at the bar of the King's Bench, his majesty's pardon for the murder of Mr. Edward Wilson in

1694, being attended, on this occasion, by the Duke of Argyle, the Earl of Mar, and several other friends.

Among the letters to and from the Countess of Suffolk is one from Mr. Law to her, then Mrs. Howard, dated Tuesday, of this tenor: "Can you not prevail on the duke to help me something more than the half year? or is there nobody that could have good nature enough to lend me one thousand pounds? I beg that if nothing of this can be done, that it may only be betwixt us two, as I take you as my great friend; and I am very well assured of it by the honor I had done me yesterday at court by the king. I had another letter yesterday from France with the same thing over again. Excuse this, dear madam, and only put yourself in my place and know at the same time that you are the only friend I have."—Wood.

(9.) "When I retired to Guermande, I had no hopes that the regent would have permitted me to leave the kingdom; I had given over all thoughts thereof when your highness sent to inform me of his intention to accord that permission, and, the next day, immediately on receiving the passports I set off. Consider, my lord, if, being in the country, removed from my papers and books, it was in my power to put in order affairs that required not only leisure, but also my presence in Paris, to arrange properly; and if it is not a piece of great injustice for the India Company to wish to take advantage of the condition to which I was reduced, and of the dishonest conduct of clerks, in requiring from me payment of sums I do not, in fact, owe, and which, even though I had been owing, were, as I have shown, expended for their service, and payable in actions or notes, of which effects belonging to me they at that time had, and still have, on their books to the amount of double or treble the sum they demand. No, my lord, I cannot bring myself to accuse the company of so much as the intention to injure me.

That company owes its birth to me. For them I have sacrificed everything, even my property and my credit, being now bankrupt, not only in France, but also in all other countries. For them I have sacrificed the interests of my children, whom I tenderly love, and who are deserving of all my affection; these children, courted by the most considerable families in France, are now destitute of fortune and of establishments. I had it in my power to have settled my daughter in marriage in the first houses of Italy, Germany, and England; but I refused all offers of that nature, thinking it inconsistent with my duty to, and my affection for, the state in whose service I had the honor to be engaged."—Wood.

CHAPTER X

Recapitulation—Comparison between this and other financial catastrophes—Reflections.

CHAPTER X

Let us recapitulate the events of the *system*, in order to review the whole and understand more clearly the causes of its downfall.

A Scotchman, going from a poor country into the midst of a rich one, had been struck with the spectacle of an extensive circulation, and had been led to think that all prosperity originated in an abundance of money. Perceiving that banks had the means of increasing the amount of money by giving to paper the currency of coin, he conceived the plan of a general bank, uniting commercial enterprises with the administration of the public revenue, issuing paper money for large payments, coin being reserved for the smaller; thus joining to the creation of an abundant circulation that of a convenient and profitable investment.

Repulsed in different countries, this Scotchman was listened to in France, where he found a government reduced to expedients and inclined to adopt new ideas. He established, at first, a private bank, which the need of an institution for credit caused to succeed. He then established, but entirely distinct from the bank, a commercial company, to which he granted privileges very different in their nature, designing to unite it with the bank eventually, and complete the vast system which he had projected. The first shares of the company were delivered to holders of different government securities which represented the floating debt, so that the creditors of the Treasury were paid with the privileges which constituted the fortune of the company. Soon, Law transferred to this company the principal leases of the revenue, on the condition that it should assume the funded debt, amounting to sixteen hundred millions. In this way all the creditors of the state were gradually to become shareholders in the company, and although they received only three percent on their capital, they would find their income increased by the profits of an immense enterprise. The project was accomplished: the sixteen hundred millions were transferred; but, managed without proper caution, they were precipitated upon the shares by the apprehension of the public that the investment would be taken up immediately. The shares rose to thirty-six times their cost, and the debt which, transformed into shares, should have been two billions at the utmost, rose to eight or ten. A universal intoxication seized the imagination of everybody. People hastened no longer to seek an investment, but to make a fortune by the marvellous rise in the value of capital. A crowd of landed proprietors sold their estates, which did not increase in value, to purchase this imaginary property, which increased in value hourly. —(Note 11.) Then the holders of the shares, better informed than those who came later, hastened to dispose of them for wealth which was real. This example was followed, and every one wished to *realize*. From this moment, the fictitious being contrasted with the real, the illusion ceased, and the decline of the shares soon became rapid. Those who had seen the fictitious capital rise to ten billions, now saw it fall to eight, and then to six billions, and gave themselves up to despair. It was proper to lament this depreciation, but not to attempt to prevent a catastrophe which had become inevitable. Law, who had permitted people to idolize him for this sudden creation of wealth, committed the fault of attempting to maintain it, and he conceived the unfortunate plan of uniting the shares to the banknotes. He attempted to establish the value of the notes by obliging the use of them in all payments above one hundred francs, and prohibiting the possession of more than five hundred francs in coin at a time. He then fixed the value of the shares in notes, and ordered that a share should be received at the bank for nine thousand francs in notes. Immediately, the shares were exchanged for this forced money, and for all kinds of property which could be bought. What followed? The imaginary capital declined in the form of notes as rapidly as it would have done in the form of shares; only the notes, which might have been saved, were sacrificed. Every one who had anything to sell refused the notes in payment, or demanded four times the value of their property. Only creditors, who were bound by their contracts, were forced to accept the notes at their full nominal value, and they were ruined. There was an attempt to reduce the nominal value on the 21st of May, in order to end this financial fiction; but a violent clamor arose, the attempt was abandoned, and the fiction was suffered to continue. The ruin of the *system* was none the less inevitable, for so monstrous an imposition could not maintain itself. The *system* must be abolished, the shares and notes converted into government securities, and the old form of the public debt resumed, after the most frightful disorders, and the ruin of so many fortunes. Such was the *system* of Law, and its sad results.

If this financial catastrophe is compared with that of the *assignats*, and of the Bank of England in the present century, a remarkable resemblance will be seen in the events of a credit system, and useful lessons can be drawn from the comparison.

Credit always anticipates the future, by employing values yet to be produced and using them as already existing.

Law, anticipating the success of a vast commercial enterprise, represented the profits of it by shares, and used them to pay the public debt.

The French revolution wished to pay for the ecclesiastical offices which had been abolished, the debt of the monarchy and the expenses of a universal war, with the national property; this property not being disposable, on account of its quantity and the want of confidence, it anticipated the sale and represented the results by papers called *assignats*.—(Note 10.)

The Bank of England, by discounts and by loans to government, anticipated and accepted as real two kinds of values; commercial bills, which represented immense quantities of colonial produce, difficult to define, and the obligations of the government, values infinitely fluctuating and depending upon the success of war and policy.

In these three cases there was a supposititious value; the shares of Law represented commercial successes and fiscal products, which were very uncertain; the *assignats* represented the price of goods, which would perhaps be diverted from their revolutionary destination; the notes of the Bank of England represented obligations which the government might not be able to fulfill.

The crisis produced by loss of confidence differed in the three cases according to the difference of circumstances. The *prestige* of a newly discovered country, the sudden displacement of an enormous sum, caused the shares of Law to rise in an extravagant manner. But a blind confidence must soon lead to a blind despair. It is well-founded confidence, based upon the real success of labor, slow in its progress, which alone is exempt from these sudden reverses which resemble tempests. The *assignats* could not be ruined in the same manner. They could not rise, because they represented the value of land, which is not susceptible of increase. But as the success of the revolution began to be distrusted, and doubts arose as to the maintenance of the national sale, they declined; and as they declined, the government, to supply the deficiency in value, was obliged to double the issue, and the repletion contributed, with the distrust, to depreciate them. The notes of the Bank of England, based upon merchandise which might depreciate, and upon engagements of the government, which the victories of France caused to diminish in value, suffered a decline, but comparatively a moderate one, because only one part of the property pledged was destructible.

In the three cases, the authorities wishing to compel confidence, met with a failure proportioned to the doubtful value of the securities, the reality of which it attempted to establish by violent measures.

Law fixed the value of the shares in notes, and attempted to fix the value of the notes themselves, by rendering the acceptance of them compulsory at a determined rate.

The revolutionary French government gave a forced currency to the *assignats*, and punished with death those who refused to take them at their nominal value.

The Bank of England was authorized to refuse to pay its notes at sight.

The result of these different measures was a deplorable disturbance in every kind of exchange. All those making bargains would not accept the depreciated money at its nominal rate, and demanded double or triple price, according to the degree of depreciation; but those who were obliged to accept payment on a previous bargain—in a word, all creditors—were ruined, because they were obliged to accept a value purely nominal.

In proportion as the resistance to the oppression increased, the authorities became more tyrannical, because they invaded domestic life. Law forbade the possession of more than five hundred francs in coin, and authorized informations. The revolutionary government, more violent and extreme in everything, established a maximum and regulated the rate of all exchanges, but succeeded no better. The Bank of England, more moderate, because the values which it proclaimed as certain were nearer the true standard, threw itself upon the patriotism of the London merchants, who assembled and declared that they would receive the notes in payments. The notes continued to circulate at a moderate discount.

But forced measures cannot prevent the fall of what must inevitably perish. The eight or ten billions of Law did not fall below what they were really worth. The *assignats*, issued beyond all proportion to the property which they represented, became utterly worthless. The Bank of England notes declined twelve and fifteen percent, and rose again after the general peace, when specie payment was resumed, but they would have succumbed if Napoleon had employed the infallible aid of time against the English policy.

Certain general truths appear from these facts.

Credit ought to represent positive values, and should be at most a very limited anticipation of these values.

As soon as values become uncertain, force can accomplish nothing to sustain them.

Forced values are refused by all who are at liberty to refuse them, and ruin those who, by previous contracts, cannot refuse them.

Thus falsehood, oppression, spoliation, destruction of all fortunes, these are the ordinary result of a false credit soon followed by a forced credit. The least deplorable of these experiences, which caused but a momentary embarrassment, that of the Bank of England, owed its safety to a successful battle. The entire wealth of a country should never depend upon the deceitful favors of fortune.

Law, unhappy man, after having made Europe resound with the name of himself and of his system, travelled through different countries, and at last took up his residence at Venice.—(Notes 1, 2.) Notwithstanding the capital which he had taken to France and that which he had left there, he ended his life in poverty.—(Notes 3-9.)

Continuing in correspondence with the Duke of Orleans, and afterward with the Duke of Bourbon, he never ceased to claim that which the French government had the injustice to refuse him. He wrote to the Duke of Bourbon, "Aesop was a model of disinterestedness, however, the courtiers accused him of keeping treasure in a trunk which he visited often; they found there only the garment which he possessed before he became a favorite of the prince. If I had saved my garment, I would not change condition with those employed in the highest places; but I am naked; they require that I shall subsist, without having any property to maintain me, and that I shall pay my debts when I have no money." Law could not obtain the old garment which he demanded. A few years after his departure from France, in 1729, he died at Venice, destitute, miserable and forgotten.

NOTES TO CHAPTER X

Law's Character – Circumstances in his Career.

(1.) He proceeded to Venice where he remained for some months, the object of the greatest curiosity to the people, who believed him to be the possessor of enormous wealth. No opinion, however, could be more erroneous. With more generosity than could have been expected from a man who, during the greatest part of his life, had been a professed gambler, he refused to enrich himself at the expense of a ruined nation. During the height of the popular frenzy for Mississippi stock, he had never doubted of the final success of his projects, in making France the richest and most powerful nation in Europe. He invested all his gains in the purchase of landed property in France—a sure proof of his own belief in the stability of his schemes. He had hoarded no plate or jewelry, and sent no money, like the dishonest jobbers, to foreign countries. His all, with the exception of one diamond, worth about five or six thousand pounds sterling, was invested in the French soil; and when he left that country, he left it almost a beggar. This fact alone ought to rescue his memory from the charge of knavery, so often and so unjustly brought against him.—Mackay.

(2.) The scandal of the time accused the regent of having

absorbed the money of the kingdom to promote his own ambitious views, and it is certain that he died seven millions in debt. Law was accused of having transferred property from France to foreign countries on his private account. He lived some time in London on the liberality of the Marquis of Lassay, and died in Venice in 1729, in a condition but little removed from indigence. I saw his widow at Brussels as humble as she had been proud and triumphant at Paris. Such revolutions are not the least useful subjects of history.—Voltaire.

(3.) It was imagined in France that he had carried away with him a large treasure. Dubois, who had become his enemy, sent a certain Abbé La Rivière with instructions to watch the slightest movements of the ex-Comptroller of the Finances. The spy could discover nothing unfavorable to him. The fact is, that Law resumed the old occupation to which he owed his first wealth, and lived by gaming, which was not discreditable at Venice.—Cochut.

(4.) He was so little attached to his property, that he offered it for distribution among those who had lost by his operations, and only wished to retain an income of 30,000 francs. This offer was admired and rejected, because people had less desire to aid the unfortunate than to destroy him.—Cochut.

(5.) Lady Law would not quit Paris until she had paid all the tradesmen's bills which the family owed.—Wood.

(6.) When Law was at the height of his power he showed most the qualities of a good minister. He abolished vexatious taxes, modified the tariff and the excise on articles where it was most burdensome to the people, recalled, by the encouragements offered by government, many Frenchmen who had been forced to expatriate themselves, liberated prisoners for debt, communicated to industry almost too great activity, undertook public works of great utility, reclaimed lands, took measures to relieve the poor—all this while the *system* was in greatest vogue, and he was most caressed and flattered.

Another real benefit, proceeding from the same inspirations, was the establishment of gratuitous instruction in the University of Paris. The Parisians were so touched by this liberality that they wished to celebrate it by a grand procession, in which all classes should be represented, even to the most humble artisan. These generous efforts, coincident with the first successes of the *system*, explain the infatuation of the nation, and justify its enthusiasm of a moment for the strange and powerful man who had produced so many phenomena.—Cochut.

(7.) He wrote, "I do not assume to myself any merit from this conduct, and I never so much as spoke upon the subject to the regent. But I cannot help observing, that this mode of behavior is diametrically opposite to the idea my enemies wish to impress to me; and surely all Europe ought to have good opinion of my disinterestedness, and of the condition to which I am reduced, since I no longer receive any proposals of marriage for my children. My lord, I conducted myself with a still greater degree of delicacy, for I took care not to have my son or my daughter married even in France, although I had the most splendid and advantageous offers of that kind. I did not choose that any part of my protection should be owing to alliance, but that it should depend solely upon the intrinsic merits of my project."—Wood.

(8.) To his moral character no compliments can be paid. His uncommon personal endowments generally ensured him success in affairs of gallantry, and to these unworthy pursuits he devoted too much of his time. Lockhart Carnwath relates that even before he left Scotland, he was "nicely expert in all manner of debaucherie." It is said that he lived several years in a course of adultery with an English lady, whom he had persuaded to elope from her husband, and to accompany him in his rambles abroad; and the Duc de Richelieu speaks in very plain terms of the attachment the Duchess Dowager of Orleans had for Mr. Law. The excess to which he carried the destructive vice of gambling has been already noticed.

Mr. Law married Lady Catharine Knollys, third daughter of Nicholas third Earl of Banbury, by his second wife Anne, daughter of William Lord Sherard. Lady Catherine, who was first married to a gentleman of the name of Lenor, by whom it does not appear she had any issue, was born 1669, and died 1747, according to the following pedigree, communicated by the late Earl of Wiltshire and Banbury:

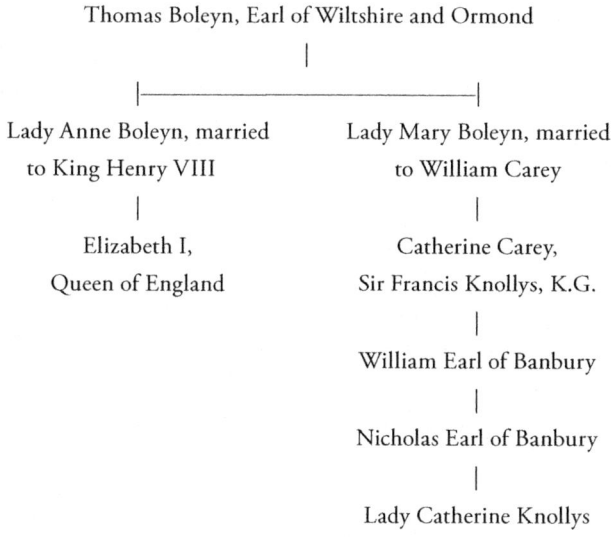

Thomas Boleyn, Earl of Wiltshire and Ormond

Lady Anne Boleyn, married to King Henry VIII

Elizabeth I, Queen of England

Lady Mary Boleyn, married to William Carey

Catherine Carey, Sir Francis Knollys, K.G.

William Earl of Banbury

Nicholas Earl of Banbury

Lady Catherine Knollys

—Wood.

(9.) Dying, he left only a few pictures, and the ring worth 10,000 (ante, Note 1.) francs, which he used to pawn when the fortune of the gaming table was unfavorable to him.

After his departure, the following genealogy of the *system* was posted on the walls of the streets of Paris: Belzebub begat Law—Law begat Mississippi—Mississippi begat the System—the System begat Paper—Paper begat the Bank—the Bank begat Banknotes—Banknotes begat Shares—Shares begat Stockbrokerage—Stockbrokerage begat the Register—the Register begat the Account—the Account begat the general Schedule—the Schedule begat Zero—from whom all power of reproduction was taken away.— Cochut.

(10.) *Assignat* was the name given to a peculiar species of paper money issued during the first French revolution. The influence of the system, operating along with the other attempts to regulate trade, forms a prominent feature in the calamitous history of the epoch. The share borne in it by the *assignats* is at the same time a memorable instance, for the use of the economist and financier, of the hopelessness of projects for creating or preserving national wealth by an issue of paper money, not the representative of available wealth and real business transactions. The first issue of *assignats* was made in the security of the forfeited ecclesiastical property, and was adopted as a preferable alternative to throwing the forfeited lands on the market, which it was no doubt judiciously believed that so large an amount of property would glut. The holder of the *assignats* might use them as money or claim the land which they represented. As more forfeitures occurred, the issue of *assignats* increased. But it soon ceased to be measured by property and was enlarged according to the exigencies of the revolutionary government. The paper money fell to half, then to a sixth part of the value of the same denomination in silver, and sinking rapidly through successive grades of decrease, silver held at last the value of one hundred and fifty times its denomination in paper. In August of 1793, 3,776 millions of francs were thus put in circulation; and virtually, the *assignats* became worthless.

(11.) "The cupidity which it (speculation) excited among all classes of people, from the very lowest up to magistrates, bishops, and even princes, distracted all attention from public affairs, and all minds from political ambitious schemes, by filling them with the fear of losing and avidity of gain. It was a new and prodigious game in which all citizens bet, one against another. Desperate gamblers will not quit their cards to annoy the government. It happened, from a series of causes perceptible only to the most experienced and most sagacious understanding, that a system entirely chimerical created a real commerce and revived the Indian Company, formerly established by the celebrated Colbert, and ruined by the wars. In fine, although there were many private fortunes ruined, the nation soon became more commercial and more rich. This system quickened the intelligence as civil war arouses the courage of a nation.

The fury for speculation was an epidemic disorder which spread into Holland and England. It merits the attention of posterity, for it was not the political interests of two or three princes which distracted nations. The people precipitated themselves into this folly, which enriched a few families and which reduced so many others to beggary."

Historians are divided in opinion as to whether they should designate Law as a knave or a madman. Both epithets were unsparingly applied to him in his lifetime, and while the unhappy consequences of his projects were still deeply felt. Posterity, however, has found reason to doubt the justice of the accusation, and to confess that John Law was neither knave nor madman, but one more deceived than deceiving, more sinned against than sinning. He was thoroughly acquainted with the philosophy and true principles of credit. He understood the monetary question better than any man of his day; and if his system fell with a crash so tremendous, it was not so much his fault as that of the people amongst whom he had erected it. He did not calculate upon the avaricious frenzy of a whole nation; he did not see that confidence, like mistrust, could be increased almost *ad infinitum*, and that hope was as extravagant as fear. How was he to foretell that the French people, like the man in the fable, would kill, in their frantic eagerness, the fine goose he had brought to lay them so many golden eggs? His fate was like that which may be supposed to have overtaken the first adventurous boatman who rowed from Erie to Ontario. Broad and smooth was the river on which he embarked; rapid and pleasant was his progress; and who was to stay him in his career? Alas, for him! the cataract was nigh. He saw, when it was too late, that the tide which wafted him so joyously along was the tide of destruction; and when he endeavored to retrace his way, he found that the current was too strong for his weak efforts to stem, and that he drew nearer, every instant, to the tremendous falls. Down he went over the sharp rocks, and the waters with him. He was dashed to pieces with his bark; but the waters, maddened and turned to foam by the rough descent, only boiled and bubbled for a time, and then flowed on again as smoothly as ever. Just so it was with Law and the French people. He was the boatman, and they were the waters.

CHAPTER XI

Preface to the Darien Expedition and the South Sea Bubble

CHAPTER XI

It seems to us appropriate, to add to the history of the Mississippi Bubble, brief accounts of the Darien Expedition and the South Sea Scheme, which were nearly contemporaneous with it, resembled it in many particulars of their progress, and afford a similar illustration of the speculative fury which, at that epoch, in their respective countries, intoxicated all classes alike, noble and humble, rich and poor, learned and ignorant.

They are unique in history for the magnitude and extent of their enterprise, for the effect they produced upon the manners and habits of the people, and for the widespread ruin in which they terminated; a result immediately disastrous to a prodigious number of individuals, but ultimately beneficial to the nation. Speculation has never, before or since, led people into such violent excesses, or brought ruin to such a number of persons of all ages, sexes and conditions; yet the same spirit pervades all countries and all times. The experience of the last thirty years in our own country, with its numerous crises, affords ample evidence of its presence here, and we hope that a history of its most remarkable manifestations in other countries may be found interesting and suggestive.

The account of the Darien Expedition is taken from the *Encyclopedia Britannica* and is the most complete and authentic which has yet been published. The history of the South Sea

Scheme is taken from Mackay's *Memoirs of Extraordinary Popular Delusions*, which contains, also, a list of the numerous absurd and monstrous projects which were eagerly embraced during the delirium of that financial fever.

CHAPTER XII

The Darien Expedition

CHAPTER XII

Of the rise, progress, and catastrophe of this ill-fated undertaking, Sir John Dalrymple, in the second volume of his *Memoirs of Great Britain and Ireland*, has given a very interesting account, authenticated in every particular by unquestionable documents. The projector and leader of the Darien Expedition was a clergyman of the name of Paterson, who, having a strong desire to see foreign countries, made his profession the means of indulging it, by going to the western world on the pretence of converting the Indians to the religion of the old. During his residence there, he became acquainted with Captain Dampier and Mr. Wafer, who afterward published, the one his voyages, the other his travels in the region where the separation is narrowest between the Atlantic and the Pacific oceans; and both of whom appear to have been men of considerable observation. But he obtained much more knowledge from men who could neither read nor write, by cultivating the acquaintance of some of the old buccaneers, who, after surviving their glories and their crimes, still, in the extremity of age and misfortune, recounted with transport the ease with which they had passed and re-passed from one sea to the other, sometimes in hundreds together, and driving strings of mules before them loaded with the plunder of friends and of foes. Paterson having examined the places, satisfied himself that on the Isthmus of Darien there was a tract of country running across from the Atlantic to the Pacific, which the Spaniards had never possessed, and inhabited by a people continually at war with them; that along the coast, on the Atlantic side, there lay a string of islands called the Sambaloes, uninhabited, and full of natural strength and of forests, from which last circumstance, one of them was called the island of the pines; that the seas there were filled with turtle and the manatee or sea cow; that midway between Porto-Bello and Carthagena, but nearly fifty leagues distant from either, at a place called Acta, in the mouth of the Darien, there was a natural harbor, capable of receiving the greatest fleets, and defended from storms by other islands which covered the mouth of it, and from enemies, by a promontory which, commanded the passage, and by hidden rocks in the passage itself; that, on the other side of the isthmus, and in the same tract of country, there were natural harbors, equally capacious and well defended; that the two oceans were connected by a ridge of lulls, which, by their height, created a temperate climate in the midst of the most sultry latitudes, and were sheltered by forests, but not rendered damp, because the trees grew at a distance from each other, and had very little underwood; that, contrary to the usual barren nature of hilly countries, the soil was of a black mold, two or three feet deep, and producing spontaneously the fine tropical fruits and plants, roots and herbs; that roads might be formed with ease along the ridge, by which mules, and even carriages, might pass from one sea to the other in the space of a day; and consequently, that this passage seemed to be pointed out by nature as a common centre to connect together the trade and intercourse of the universe.

Paterson knew that ships which stretch in a straight line from one point to another, and with one wind, run less risks and require fewer hands, than ships which pass through many latitudes, follow the windings of many coasts, and require many winds; that vessels of seven or eight hundred tons burden are often to be met in the South Sea, navigated by not more than eight or ten hands, because these hands have little else to do than set their sails when they begin their voyage, and to take them in when they end it; that as soon as ships from Britain should get so far south as to reach the trade-wind, which seldom varies, that wind would carry them to Darien, and the same wind would carry ships from the Bay of Panama, on the opposite side of the isthmus, to the East Indies; that as soon as ships coming from the East Indies to the Bay of Panama got so far north as the latitude of 40°, to reach the westerly winds, which about that latitude blow almost as regularly from the west as the trade-winds do from the east, these winds would carry them in the track of the Spanish Acapulco ships to the coast of Mexico, whence the land-wind, which blows forever from the north to the south, would carry them along the coast of Mexico into the Bay of Panama. Thus, in going from Britain, ships would encounter no uncertain winds except during their passage south into the latitude of the trade-wind; and in coming from India to the Bay of Panama they would meet no uncertain winds, except in their passage north to the latitude of the westerly winds, and in going from the other side of the isthmus to the east, with no uncertain wind whatsoever. Gold was seen by Paterson in some places on the isthmus; and hence, an island on the Atlantic side was called the Gold Island, and a river on the side running to the Pacific was called the Golden River; but these were objects which he regarded not at that time, because far greater were in his eye, namely, the shortening of distances, the drawing of nations nearer to each other, the preservation of the valuable lives of seamen, and the saving in freight and in time, so important to merchants, and to an animal whose life is of so short duration as that of man.—(Note 1.)

By this obscure Scotchman a project was formed to settle,

on this neglected spot, a great and powerful colony; not as other colonies have, for the most part, been settled, by chance, and unprotected by the country whence they proceeded; but by system, upon foresight, and to receive the ample protection of those governments to whom he was to offer his project. And certainly no greater idea has been formed since the time of Columbus.

Paterson's original intention was to submit his project to England, as the country which had most interest in it, not only from the benefit common to all nations, of shortening the length of voyages to the East Indies, but by the effect which it would have had in connecting the interest of her European, West Indian, American, African, and East Indian trade. Paterson, however, having few acquaintances, and no protection in London, thought of drawing the public eye upon him, and ingratiating himself with moneyed men and with great men, by assisting them to model a project, which was at that time in embryo, for erecting the Bank of England. But that happened to him which has happened to many projectors in his situation; the persons to whom he applied, made use of his ideas, took the credit of them to themselves, were civil to him for a while, and neglected him afterward. He therefore communicated his project of a colony only to a few persons in London, and these few discouraged him.

He next submitted his project to the Dutch, the Hamburgers, and the Elector of Brandenburg; because, by means of the passage of the Rhine and Elbe through their states, he thought that the great additional quantities of East Indian and American goods his colony would export to Europe would be distributed throughout Germany. The Dutch and Hamburg merchants, although they had most interest in the project, heard him with indifference; while the elector, who had very little interest in it, received him with honor and kindness; but court arts and false reports soon lost him even that prince's favor. Paterson, on his return to London, formed a friendship with Mr. Fletcher, of Saltown, whose mind was inflamed with the love of public good, and all whose ideas to procure it had a sublimity about them. Fletcher brought Paterson down to Scotland, presented him to the Marquis of Tweeddale, then minister for that country; and thereafter, with that power which a vehement spirit always possesses over a diffident one, persuaded the marquis, by arguments of public good and the honor which would redound to his administration, to adopt the project. Lord Stair and Mr. Johnston, the two secretaries of state, patronized those abilities in Paterson which they possessed in themselves; and the lord advocate, Sir James Stuart, the same person who had adjusted the Prince of Orange's declaration at the revolution, and whose son had married a niece of Lord Stair, went naturally along with his connections. These persons, in June, 1695, procured a statute from parliament, and afterward a charter from the crown in terms thereof, "for creating a trading company to Africa and the New World, with power to plant colonies and build forts, by consent of the inhabitants, in places not possessed by other European nations."

Peterson, now finding the ground firm under him, and that he was supported by almost all the power and talents of his country, the character of Fletcher, and the sanction of an act of parliament and royal charter, threw his project boldly before the public, and opened a subscription for a company. The frenzy of the Scotch nation to sign the Solemn League and Covenant never exceeded the rapidity with which they ran to subscribe to the Darien Company. The nobility, the gentry, the merchants, the people, the royal burghs, without the exception of one, and most of the other public bodies, subscribed. Young women threw their little fortunes into the stock; and widows sold their jointures to get the command of money for the same purpose.

Almost immediately £400,000 were subscribed in Scotland, although there was not at that time above £800,000 of cash in the kingdom. The famous Mr. Law, then a youth, afterward confessed that the facility with which he saw the passion of speculation communicate itself, satisfied him of the possibility of producing the same effect by means of the same cause, but upon a larger scale, when the Duke of Orleans engaged him against his will to turn his bank into a bubble. Paterson's project, which had been received by strangers with fears when opened to them in private, filled them with hopes when it came to them upon the wings of public fame; for Colonel Erskine, son of Lord Cardrose, and Mr. Heldane of Gleneaghs, the one a generous branch of a generous stem, and the other a country gentleman of fortune and character, having been deputed to receive subscriptions in England and on the continent, the English subscribed £300,000, and the Dutch and Hamburgers £200,000.— (Note 2.)

In the meantime, the jealousy of trade, which has done more mischief to the commerce of England than all other causes put together, created an alarm in England; and the Houses of Lords and Commons, without previous inquiry or reflection, on the 13th of December, 1695, concurred in a joint address to the king against the establishment of the Darien Company, as detrimental to the interest of the East India Company. Soon afterward the Commons impeached some of their own countrymen for being instrumental in erecting the company, and also some of the Scotch nation, one of whom was Lord Belhaven; that is to say, they arraigned the subjects of another country for making use of their own laws. Among six hundred legislators, not one had the sense, not to say genius, to propose a committee of both parliaments to inquire into the principles and consequences of the establishment; and if these should, upon inquiry, be found sound and beneficial, that the advantage should be communicated, by a participation of rights, to both nations. The king's answer was, that he had been ill-advised in Scotland. He soon afterward changed his Scottish ministers, and sent orders to his residents at Hamburg to present a memorial to the senate, in which he disowned the company, and warned them against all connections with it. The senate transmitted the memorial to the assembly of merchants, who returned it with the following spirited answer: "We look upon it as a very strange thing, that the king of Britain should offer to hinder us, who are a free people, to trade with whom we please; but are amazed to think that he would hinder us from joining with his own subjects in Scotland, to whom he had lately given such large privileges, by so solemn an act of parliament." But the merchants, seeing the scheme discouraged by their governments, were soon intimidated; and the Dutch, Hamburg, and London merchants withdrew their subscriptions.—(Notes 3 and 4.)

The Scotch, not discouraged, were rather animated by this oppression; for they converted it into a proof of the envy of the English, and of their consciousness of the great advantages which were to flow to Scotland from the colony. The company proceeded to build six ships in Holland, from thirty-six to sixty guns, and they engaged 1,200 men for the colony; amongst whom were younger sons of many of the noble and ancient families of Scotland and sixty officers who had been disbanded at the peace, who carried with them such of their private men, generally raised on their own or the estates of their relations, as they knew to be faithful and brave, most of them being Highlanders. The Scotch parliament, on the 6th of August, 1698, unanimously addressed the king to support the company. The lord president, Sir Hugh Dalrymple, brother of Lord Stair, and head of the bench, and the lord advocate Sir James Stuart, head of the bar, jointly drew up memorials to the king, able in point of argument, information, and arrangement, in which they defended the rights of the company upon the principles of constitutional and of public law; and neighboring nations, with a mixture of surprise and respect, saw the poorest kingdom of Europe sending forth the most gallant and the most numerous colony which had ever set out from the old to the new world. On the 26th day of July, 1698, the whole city of Edinburgh poured down to Leith to see the colony depart, amidst the tears, and prayers, and praises of relations, and friends and countrymen. Many seamen and soldiers, whose services had been refused, because more had offered themselves than were needed, were found hid in the ships, and, when ordered ashore, clung to the ropes and timbers, imploring to go without reward along with their companions. Twelve hundred men sailed in five stout ships, and arrived at Darien in two months, with the loss of only fifteen of their people. At that time it was in their power, most of them being well born, and all of them hardily bred and inured to the fatigues and dangers of the late war, to have marched from the northmost part of Mexico to the southmost point of Chile, and to have overturned the whole empire of Spain in South America. But, modest respecting their own and their country's character, and afraid of its being alleged that they had plunder, and not a settlement in view, they began with purchasing lands from the natives, and sending messages of amity to the Spanish governors within their reach; and then fixed their station at Acta, calling it New St. Andrew, from the name of the titular saint of Scotland, and the country itself New Caledonia. One of the sides of the harbor being formed by a long narrow neck of land which ran into the sea, they cut it across so as to join the ocean and harbor. Within this defence they erected their fort, planting upon it fifty pieces of cannon. On the other side of the harbor there was a mountain about a mile in height, on which they placed a watch-house, which, in the rarefied air within the tropics, so favorable for vision, gave them an immense range of prospect, in order to prevent all surprise. To this place it was observed that the Highlanders often repaired to enjoy the cool air, and to talk of their friends whom they had left behind on their native hills. The first public act of the colony was to publish a declaration of freedom of trade and religion to all nations. This luminous idea originated with Paterson.

But the Dutch East India Company having pressed the king, in concurrence with his English subjects, to prevent the settlement at Darien, orders had been sent from England to the governors of the West Indian and American colonies, to issue proclamations against giving assistance, or even holding correspondence with the colony; and these were more or less harshly expressed, according to the temper of the different governors. The Scotch, trusting to far different treatment and to the supplies which they expected from these colonies, had not brought sufficient provisions along with them, and fell into diseases from bad or inadequate food; but the more generous savages, by hunting and fishing for them, afforded them that relief which fellow Britons had refused. They lingered eight months, waiting in vain for assistance from Scotland and almost all of them either died out or quitted the settlement. Paterson, who had been the first to enter the ship at Leith, was the last to go on board at Darien.

During the space of two years, while the establishment of his colony had been in agitation, Spain had made no complaint to England or Scotland against it. The Darien council even averred in their papers, which are in the Advocates' Library, that the right of the company was debated before the king, in presence of the Spanish ambassador, ere the colony left Scotland. But now, on the 3rd of May, 1698, the Spanish ambassador at London presented a memorial to the king, in which he complained of the settlement at Darien as an encroachment on the rights of his master.—(Notes 5, 6 and 7.)

The Scotch, ignorant of the misfortunes of their colony, but provoked at this memorial, soon afterward sent out another colony of 1,300 men, to support an establishment which was now no more; but this last proved unlucky in its passage. One of the vessels was lost at sea, many men died on board, and the rest arrived at different times, broken in their health, and disappointed when they heard the fate of those who had gone before them. Added to the misfortunes of the first colony, the second had a misfortune peculiar to itself. The General Assembly of the church of Scotland sent out four ministers, with orders to take charge of the souls of the colony, and to erect a presbytery, with a moderator, clerk, and record of proceedings; to appoint ruling elders, deacons, overseers of the manners of the people, and assistants in the exercise of church discipline and government, and to hold regular kirk-sessions. When they arrived, the officers and gentlemen were occupied in building houses for themselves with their own hands, because there was no assistance to be got from others; yet the four ministers complained grievously that the council did not order houses to be immediately built for their accommodation. They had not had the precaution to bring with them letters of recommendation from the directors at home to the council abroad; and on these accounts, not meeting with all the attention they expected from the higher, they paid court to the inferior ranks of the colonists, and by this means sowed divisions in the colony. They exhausted the spirits of the people, by requiring their attendance at sermon four or five hours at a time, relieving each other by preaching alternately, but allowing no relief whatever to their hearers. The employment of one of the days set aside for religious exercise, which was Wednesday they divided into three parts; thanksgiving, humiliation, and supplication, in which three ministers followed one another. And as the service of the church of Scotland, consists of a lecture with a comment, a sermon, two prayers, three psalms, and a blessing, the work of the day, upon an average of the length of the service in that age, could not occupy less than twelve hours, during which time the colony was collected, and kept crowded together in the guard-room which was used as a church, in a tropical climate, and in a sickly season. The preachers presented a paper to the council, which they took care to make public, requiring them to set aside a day for solemn fasting and humiliation; and, under pretence of enumerating the sins of the people, they poured out abuse on their rulers. They damped the courage of the people by continually representing hell as the termination of life to most men, because most men are sinners. Carrying the presbyterian doctrine of predestination to an extreme, they put a stop to all exertions, by showing that the consequences of these depended not on the individuals by whom they were made, but on an all-controlling and irresistible power, by which, independently of human efforts and volitions, every thing was necessarily determined. They converted the numberless accidents to which soldiers and seamen are exposed into immediate judgments of God against their sins; and having resolved to quit the settlement, they, in excuse for doing so, wrote bitter letters to the general assembly against the characters of the colonists, and the advantages of the colony itself.

One of these men, in a kind of history of the colony which he published, exulted with a savage triumph over the misfortunes of his countrymen. "They were such a rude company," said he, "that I believe Sodom never declared such impudence in sinning as they. An observant eye might see that they were running the way they went; hell and judgment was to be seen upon them, and in them, before the time. Their cup was full; it could hold no more: they were ripe; they must be cut down with the sickle of the wrath of God." The last party which joined the second colony at Darien, after it had been three months settled, was Captain Campbell of Finab, with a company of the people of his own estate, whom he had commanded in Flanders, and whom he carried to Darien in his own ship. On their arrival at New St. Andrew, they found that intelligence had been received that a Spanish force of 1,600 men, which had been brought from the coast of the South Sea, lay encamped at Tubucantee, waiting there till a Spanish squadron of eleven ships which was expected should arrive, when they were jointly to attack the fort. The military command was offered to Captain Campbell, in compliment to his reputation and to his birth as a descendant of the families Broadalbane and Athol. In order to prevent a joint attack, he resolved to attack first; and therefore on the second day after his arrival, he marched with two hundred men to Tubucantee, before his approach could be known to the enemy, stormed the camp in the night-time, dissipated the Spanish force with much slaughter, and returned to the fort the fifth day. But he found the Spanish ships off the harbor, their troops landed, and almost all hope of aid or of provisions cut off; yet he stood a siege of nearly six weeks, until almost all the officers had died. The enemy, by their approaches, had cut off his well, and his ammunition had been so far expended that he was obliged to melt the pewter dishes of the garrison into balls. The garrison then capitulated, and obtained not only the common honors of war and security for the property of the company, but as if they had been conquerors, even exacted hostages for the performance of the conditions. Captain Campbell alone desired to be excepted from the capitulation, saying that he was sure the Spaniards would not forgive him the mischief which he so lately had done them. But the brave, by their courage, often escape that death which they seem to provoke. Captain Campbell made his escape in his vessel, and arrived safely at New York, whence he proceeded to Scotland, where the company presented him with a gold medal, in which his bravery was duly commemorated. The lord-lyon king-at-arms, whose office it is in Scotland to confer badges of distinction upon honorable actions according to the rules of heraldry, also granted him a Highlander and an Indian as supporters to his coat of arms.

But a harder fate attended those whom Captain Campbell had left at Darien. They were so weak in their health as not to be able to weigh up the anchors of the Rising Sun, one of their ships, which carried sixty guns; the generous Spaniards, however, assisted them. In going out of the harbor the vessel ran aground. The prey was tempting; and, to obtain it, the Spaniards had only to stand by and look on; but they showed that mercy to the Scotch in distress, which one of their own countrymen, General Elliot, afterward returned to the posterity of these Spaniards at the siege of Gibraltar. The Darien ships being leaky and weakly manned, were obliged in their voyage to take shelter in different ports belonging to Spain and England. But the Spaniards in the new world treated them with uniform kindness, while the English governments showed them none; and one of their ships was seized and detained. In fact, only Captain Campbell's ship and another small one were saved. The Rising Sun was lost on the bar of Charlestown; and of the colony, not more than thirty, saved from war, shipwreck, or disease, ever returned to their native country.—(Note 8.)

Paterson, who had withstood the blow, could not endure the reflection of misfortune. He was seized with a lunacy in his passage home, after the ruin of the first colony; but he recovered in his own country, where his spirit, still ardent and unbroken, presented a new plan to the company, founded on the idea of King William, that England should have the joint dominion of the settlement with Scotland. He survived many years in Scotland, pitied, respected, but neglected. After the union of the two kingdoms, he claimed reparation of his losses from the equivalent money obtained by England to the Darien Company, but was paid nothing; because a grant to him from a public fund would have been only an act of humanity, and not a political job. Thus ended the colony of Darien; an adventure which, in its disastrous results, inflicted a severe blow upon Scotland, and excited feelings of deep hostility toward the English government and nation, which half a century was scarcely sufficient to extinguish.

NOTES TO CHAPTER XII

(1.) The time and expense of navigation to China, Japan, the Spice Islands, and the far greatest part of the East Indies, will be lessened more than half, and the consumption of European commodities and manufactures will soon be more than doubled. Trade will increase trade, and money will beget money, and the trading world shall need no more to want work for their hands, but will rather want hands for their work. Thus, this door of the seas, and the key of the universe, with anything of a reasonable management, will, of course, enable its proprietors to give laws to both oceans and to become arbitrators of the commercial world, without being liable to the fatigues, expenses, and dangers, or contracting the guilt and blood of Alexander and Caesar. In all our empires, that have been anything universal, the conquerors have been obliged to seek out and court their conquests from afar; but the universal force and influence of this attractive magnet is such, as can much more effectually bring empire home to its proprietors' doors. But, from what hath been said, you may easily perceive that the nature of these discoveries is such as not to he engrossed by any one nation or people, with exclusion to others; nor can it be thus attempted without evident hazard and ruin, as we see in the case of Spain and Portugal, who, by their prohibiting any other people to trade, or so much as go to or dwell in the Indies, have not only lost that trade they were not able to maintain, but have depopulated and ruined their countries therewith; so that the Indies have rather conquered Spain and Portugal than they have conquered the Indies; for, by their permitting all to go out, and none to come in. they have not only lost the people which are gone to these remote and luxuriant regions, but such as remain are become wholly unprofitable and good for nothing. Thus, not unlike the case of the dog in the fable, they have lost their own countries, and yet not gotten the Indies. People and their industry are the true riches of a prince or nation; and in respect to them, all other things are imaginary. This was well understood by the people of Rome, who, contrary to the maxims of Sparta and Spain, by general naturalizations, liberty of conscience, and immunity of government, far more effectually and advantageously conquered and kept the world than ever they did, or possibly could have done, by the sword.—Dalrymple's *Extracts from Paterson's own Papers*.

Enthusiasm of the Scotch

(2.) That extraordinary projector (Paterson) had transported the ordinary cool and calculating Scots almost out of their senses. From high to low, all his countrymen were visited by day-dreams of sudden and enormous wealth, by visions of gold, and of nothing but gold. The new company, which included some of the noblest and most intellectual of the Scottish nation, had caused six stout ships to be built in Holland, and many of the aristocracy had embarked their younger sons, confident that they were putting them on the sure road to wealth and distinction. Several lords denuded their estates to send out their vassals and tenantry; and many officers who had been disbanded by the late peace had ventured their persons and their little property.—*Pict. Hist. of Eng.*, vol. iv. p. 95.

Difficulties at the Start

(3.) The clamor in Scotland increased against the ministry, who had disowned their company, and in a great measure defeated their design, from which they had promised themselves such heaps of treasure. . . . At Madeira they took in a supply of wine, and then returned to Crab Island, in the neighborhood of St. Thomas, lying between Santa Cruz and Porto Rico. Their design was to take possession of this little island; but when they entered the road, they saw a large tent pitched upon the strand, and the Danish colors flying. Finding themselves anticipated in this quarter, they directed their course to the coast of Darien.—Smollett.

Opposition of the English

(4.) They represented that, in consequence of the exemption from taxes, and other advantages granted to the Scottish company, that kingdom would become a free port for all East and West India commodities; that the Scots would be enabled to supply all Europe at a cheaper rate than the English could afford to sell their merchandise for; therefore, England would lose the benefit of its foreign trade; besides, they observed that the Scots would smuggle their commodities into England, to the great detriment of his majesty and his customs.—*Ibid.*

(5.) But there was another cause more powerful than the remonstrances of the Spanish court, to which this colony fell a sacrifice; and that was, the jealousy of the English traders and planters. . . . The English apprehended that their planters would be allured into this new colony by the double prospect of finding gold and plundering the Spaniards, and that the settlement would produce a rupture with Spain; in consequence of which, the English effects in that kingdom would be confiscated.—*Ibid.*

Opposition of the Dutch

(6.) The Dutch, too, are said to have been jealous of the company, which, in time, might have proved their competitors in the illicit commerce to the Spanish main, and to have hardened the king's heart against the new settlers.—*Ibid.*

(7.) It was further given out, to raise the national disgust yet higher, that the opposition the king gave to the Scotch colony flowed neither from a regard to the interests of England, nor to the treaties with Spain, but from a care, of the Dutch, who, from Curacoa, drove a coasting trade among the Spanish plantations with great advantage; which, they said, the Scotch colony, if once settled, would draw only away from them.—Burnet.

Disastrous Result

(8.) Thus vanished all the golden dreams of the Scottish nation, which had engaged in this design with incredible eagerness, and even embarked a greater sum of money than ever they had advanced upon any other occasion. They were now not only disappointed in their expectations of wealth and affluence, but a great number of families were absolutely ruined by the miscarriage of the design, which they imputed solely to the conduct of King William. The whole kingdom of Scotland seemed to join in the clamor that was raised against their sovereign, taxed him with double-dealing, inhumanity, and base ingratitude, to a people who had lavished their treasure and best blood in support of his government and in the gratification of his ambition; and had their power been equal to their animosity, in all probability a rebellion would have ensued.—Smollett.

CHAPTER XIII

The South Sea Bubble

At length corruption, like a general flood,
Did deluge all; and avarice creeping on,
Spread, like a low-born mist, and hid the sun.
Statesmen and patriots plied alike the stocks,
Peeress and butler shared alike the box;
And judges jobbed, and bishops bit the town,
And mighty dukes packed cards for half-a-crown:
Britain was sunk in lucre's sordid charms.

Alexander Pope

CHAPTER XIII

The South Sea Company was originated by the celebrated Harley, Earl of Oxford, in the year 1711, with the view of restoring public credit, which had suffered by the dismissal of the whig ministry, and of providing for the discharge of the army and navy debentures, and other parts of the floating debt, amounting to nearly ten millions sterling. A company of merchants, at that time without a name, took this debt upon themselves, and the government agreed to secure them for a certain period the interest of six percent. To provide for this interest, amounting to £600,000 per annum, the duties upon wines, vinegar, India goods, wrought silks, tobacco, whale-fins, and some other articles, were rendered permanent. The monopoly of the trade to the South Seas was granted, and the company, being incorporated by act of parliament, assumed the title by which it has ever since been known. The minister took great credit to himself for his share in this transaction, and the scheme was always called by his flatterers "the Earl of Oxford's masterpiece."

Even at this early period of its history, the most visionary ideas were formed by the company and the public of the immense riches of the eastern coast of South America. Everybody had heard of the gold and silver mines of Peru and Mexico; every one believed them to be inexhaustible, and that it was only necessary to send the manufactures of England to the coast to be repaid a hundred fold in gold and silver ingots by the natives. A report industriously spread, that Spain was willing to concede four ports on the coasts of Chile and Peru for the purposes of traffic, increased the general confidence, and for many years the South Sea Company's stock was in high favor.

Philip V of Spain, however, never had any intention of admitting the English to a free trade in the ports of Spanish America. Negotiations were set on foot, but their only result was the assiento contract, or the privilege of supplying the colonies with negroes for thirty years, and of sending once a year a vessel, limited both as to tonnage and value of cargo, to trade with Mexico, Peru, or Chile. The latter permission was only granted upon the hard condition, that the king of Spain should enjoy one-fourth of the profits, and a tax of five percent, on the remainder. This was a great disappointment to the Earl of Oxford and his party, who were reminded much oftener than they found agreeable, of the

"Parturiunt montes, nascitur ridiculus mus."

But the public confidence in the South Sea Company was not shaken. The Earl of Oxford declared that Spain would permit two ships, in addition to the annual ship, to carry out merchandise during the first year; and a list was published, in which all the ports and harbors of these coasts were pompously set forth as open to the trade of Great Britain. The first voyage of the annual ship was not made till the year 1717, and in the following year the trade was suppressed by the rupture with Spain.

The king's speech at the opening of the session of 1717, made pointed allusion to the state of public credit, and recommended that proper measures should be taken to reduce the national debt.

The two great monetary corporations, the South Sea Company and the Bank of England, made proposals to parliament on the 20th of May ensuing. The South Sea Company prayed that their capital stock of ten millions might be increased to twelve, by subscription or otherwise, and offered to accept five percent, instead of six, upon the whole amount. The bank made proposals equally advantageous. The House debated for some time, and finally three acts were passed, called the South Sea Act, the Bank Act, and the General Fund Act. By the first, the proposals of the South Sea Company were accepted, and that body held itself ready to advance the sum of two millions toward discharging the principal and interest of the debt due by the state for the four lottery funds of the ninth and tenth years of Queen Anne. By the second act, the bank received a lower rate of interest for the sum of £1,775,027 15s. due to it by the state, and agreed to deliver up to be cancelled as many exchequer bills as amounted to two millions sterling, and to accept of an annuity of one hundred thousand pounds, being after the rate of five percent, the whole redeemable at one year's notice. They were further required to be ready to advance, in case of need, a sum not exceeding £2,500,000 upon the same terms of five percent, interest, redeemable by parliament. The General Fund Act recited the various deficiencies, which were to be made good by the aids derived from the foregoing sources.

The name of the South Sea Company was thus continually before the public. Though their trade with the South American States produced little or no augmentation of their revenues, they continued to flourish as a monetary corporation. Their stock was in high request, and the directors, buoyed up with success, began to think of new means for extending their influence. The Mississippi scheme of John Law, which so dazzled and captivated the French people, inspired them with an idea that they could carry on the same game in England. The anticipated failure of his plans did not divert them from their intention. Wise in their own conceit, they imagined they could avoid his faults, carry on their schemes forever, and stretch the cord of credit to its extremest tension, without causing it to snap asunder.

It was while Law's plan was at its greatest height of popularity, while people were crowding in thousands to the Rue Quincampoix, and ruining themselves with frantic eagerness, that the South Sea directors laid before parliament their famous plan for paying off the national debt. Visions of boundless wealth floated before the fascinated eyes of the people in the two most celebrated countries of Europe. The English commenced their career of extravagance somewhat later than the French; but as soon as the delirium seized them they were determined not to be outdone. Upon the 22nd of January, 1720, the House of Commons resolved itself into a committee of the whole House, to take into consideration that part of the king's speech at the opening of the session which related to the public debts, and the proposal of the South Sea Company toward the redemption and sinking of the same. The proposal set forth at great length, and under several heads, the debts of the state, amounting to £30,981,712, which the company were anxious to take upon themselves, upon consideration of five percent, per annum, secured to them until Midsummer, 1727; after which time, the whole was to become redeemable at the pleasure of the legislature, and the interest to be reduced to four percent. The proposal was received with great favor; but the Bank of England had many friends in the House of Commons, who were desirous that that body should share in the advantages that were likely to accrue. On behalf of this corporation it was represented, that they had performed great and eminent services to the state in the most difficult times, and deserved, at least, that if any advantage was to be made by public bargains of this nature, they should be preferred before a company that had never done anything for the nation. The further consideration of the matter was accordingly postponed for five days. In the meantime a plan was drawn up by the governors of the bank. The South Sea Company, afraid that the bank might offer still more advantageous terms to the government than themselves, reconsidered their former proposal, and made some alterations in it, which they hoped would render it more acceptable. The principal change was a stipulation that the government might redeem these debts at the expiration of four years, instead of seven, as at first suggested. The bank resolved not to be outbidden in this singular auction, and the governors also reconsidered their first proposal, and sent in a new one.

Thus, each corporation having made two proposals, the House began to deliberate. Mr. Robert Walpole was the chief speaker in favor of the bank, and Mr. Aislabie, the Chancellor of the Exchequer, the principal advocate on behalf of the South Sea Company. It was resolved, on the 2nd of February, that the proposals of the latter were most advantageous to the country. They were accordingly received, and leave was given to bring in a bill to that effect.

Exchange Alley was in a fever of excitement. The company's stock, which had been at a hundred and thirty the previous day, gradually rose to three hundred, and continued to rise with the most astonishing rapidity during the whole time that the bill in its several stages was under discussion. Mr. Walpole was almost the only statesman in the House who spoke out boldly against it. He warned them, in eloquent and solemn language, of the evils that would ensue. It countenanced, he said, "the dangerous practice of stock-jobbing, and would divert the genius of the nation from trade and industry. It would hold out a dangerous lure to decoy the unwary to their ruin, by making them part with the earnings of their labor for a prospect of imaginary wealth. The great principle of the project was an evil of first-rate magnitude; it was to raise artificially the value of the stock, by exciting and keeping up a general infatuation, and by promising dividends out of funds which could never be adequate to the purpose." In a prophetic spirit he added, that if the plan succeeded, the directors would become masters of the government, form a new and absolute aristocracy in the kingdom, and control the resolutions of the legislature. If it failed, which he was convinced it would, the result would bring general discontent and ruin upon the country. Such would be the delusion, that when the evil day came, as come it would, the people would start up, as from a dream, and ask themselves if these things could have been true. All his eloquence was in vain. He was looked upon as a false prophet, or compared to the hoarse raven, croaking omens of evil. His friends, however, compared him to Cassandra, predicting evils which would only be believed when they came borne to men's hearths, and stared them in the face at their own boards. Although, in former times, the House had listened with the utmost attention to every word that fell from his lips, the benches became deserted when it was known that he would speak on the South Sea question.

The bill was two months in its progress through the House of Commons. During this time every exertion was made by the directors and their friends, and more especially by the chairman, the noted Sir John Blunt, to raise the price of the stock. The most extravagant rumors were in circulation. Treaties between England and Spain were spoken of, whereby the latter was to grant a free trade to all her colonies; and the rich produce of the mines of Potosi-la-Paz was to be brought to England until silver should become almost as plentiful as iron. For cotton and woollen goods, which could be supplied to them in abundance, the dwellers in Mexico were to empty their golden mines. The company of merchants trading to the South Seas would be the richest the world ever saw, and every hundred pounds invested in it would produce hundreds per annum to the stockholder. At last the stock was raised by these means to near four hundred; but, after fluctuating a good deal, settled at three hundred and thirty, at which price it remained when the bill passed the Commons by a majority of 172 against 55.—(Note 1.)

In the House of Lords the bill was hurried through all its stages with unexampled rapidity. On the 4th of April it was read a first time; on the 5th, it was read a second time; on the 6th, it was committed; and on the 7th, was read a third time and passed.

Several peers spoke warmly against the scheme; but their warnings fell upon dull, cold ears. A speculating frenzy had seized them as well as the plebeians. Lord North and Grey said the bill was unjust in its nature, and might prove fatal in its consequences, being calculated to enrich the few and impoverish the many. The Duke of Wharton followed; but, as he only retailed at second-hand the arguments so eloquently stated by Walpole in the Lower House, he was not listened to with even the same attention that had been bestowed upon Lord North and Grey. Earl Cowper followed on the same side, and compared the bill to the famous horse of the siege of Troy. Like that, it was ushered in and received with great pomp and acclamations of joy, but bore within it treachery and destruction. The Earl of Sunderland endeavored to answer all objections; and on the question being put, there appeared only seventeen peers against, and eighty-three in favor of the project. The very same day, on which it passed the Lords, it received the royal assent, and became the law of the land.

It seemed at that time as if the whole nation had turned stockjobbers. Exchange Alley was every day blocked up by crowds, and Cornhill was impassable for the number of carriages. Everybody came to purchase stock. "Every fool aspired to be a knave." In the words of a ballad published at the time, and sung about the streets,[1]

> *Then stars and garters did appear*
> *Among the meaner rabble;*
> *To buy and sell, to see and hear*
> *The Jews and Gentiles squabble.*
>
> *The greatest ladies thither came,*
> *And plied in chariots daily,*
> *Or pawned their jewels for a sum*
> *To venture in the Alley.*

The inordinate thirst of gain that had afflicted all ranks of society was not to be slaked even in the South Sea. Other schemes, of the most extravagant kind, were started. The sharelists were speedily filled up, and an enormous traffic carried on in shares, while, of course, every means were resorted to, to raise them to an artificial value in the market.

Contrary to all expectation, South Sea stock fell when the bill received the royal assent. On the 7th of April the shares were quoted at three hundred and ten, and on the following day at two hundred and ninety. Already the directors had tasted the profits of their scheme, and it was not likely that they should quietly allow the stock to find its natural level without an effort to raise it. Immediately their busy emissaries were set to work. Every person interested in the success of the project endeavored to draw a knot of listeners around him, to whom he expatiated on the treasures of the South American seas. Exchange Alley was crowded with attentive groups. One rumor alone, asserted

---

[1]. A South-Sea Ballad; or, Merry Remarks upon Exchange Alley Bubbles. To a new tune called "The Grand Elixir; or, the Philosopher's Stone discovered."

with the utmost confidence, had an immediate effect upon the stock. It was said that Earl Stanhope had received overtures in France from the Spanish government to exchange Gibraltar and Port Mahon for some places on the coast of Peru, for the security and enlargement of the trade in the South Seas. Instead of one annual ship trading to those ports, and allowing the king of Spain twenty-five percent, out of the profits, the company might build and charter as many ships as they pleased, and pay no percentage whatever to any foreign potentate,

"Visions of ingots danced before their eyes,"

and stock rose rapidly. On the 12th of April, five days after the bill had become law, the directors opened their books for a subscription of a million, at the rate of £300 for every £100 capital. Such was the concourse of persons of all ranks, that this first subscription was found to amount to above two millions of original stock. It was to be paid in five payments, of £60 each for every £100. In a few days the stock advanced to three hundred and forty, and the subscriptions were sold for double the price of the first payment. To raise the stock still higher, it was declared, in a general court of directors, on the 21st of April, that the midsummer dividend should be ten percent, and that all subscriptions should be entitled to the same. These resolutions answering the end designed, the directors, to improve the infatuation of the moneyed men, opened their books for a second subscription of a million, at four hundred percent. Such was the frantic eagerness of people of every class to speculate in these funds, that in the course of a few hours no less than a million and a half was subscribed at that rate.—(Notes 7, 8.)

In the meantime, innumerable joint-stock companies started up everywhere. They soon received the name of Bubbles, the most appropriate that imagination could devise. The populace are often most happy in the nicknames they employ. None could be more apt than that of Bubbles. Some of them lasted for a week or a fortnight, and were no more heard of, while others could not even live out that short span of existence. Every evening produced new schemes, and every morning new projects. The highest of the aristocracy were as eager in this hot pursuit of gain as the most plodding jobber in Cornhill. The Prince of Wales became governor of one company, and is said to have cleared £40,000, by his speculations.[2] The Duke of Bridgewater started a scheme for the improvement of London and Westminster, and the Duke of Chandos another. There were nearly a hundred different projects, each more extravagant and deceptive than the other. To use the words of the "Political State," they were "set on foot and promoted by crafty knaves, then pursued by multitudes of covetous fools, and at last appeared to be, in effect, what their vulgar appellation denoted them to be—bubbles and mere cheats." It was computed that near one million and a half sterling was won and lost by these unwarrantable practices, to the impoverishment of many a fool, and the enriching of many a rogue.

Some of these schemes were plausible enough, and, had they been undertaken at a time when the public mind was unexcited, might have been pursued with advantage to all concerned. But they were established merely with a view of raising the shares in the market. The projectors took the first opportunity of a rise to sell out, and next morning the scheme was at an end. Maitland, in his *History of London*, gravely informs us, that one of the projects which received great encouragement, was for the establishment of a company "to make deal boards out of sawdust." This is no doubt intended as a joke; but there is abundance of evidence to show that dozens of schemes, hardly a whit more

---

2. Coxe's *Walpole*, Correspondence between Mr. Secretary Craggs and Earl Stanhope,—(Note 5.)

reasonable, lived their little day, ruining hundreds ere they fell. One of them was for a wheel for perpetual motion—capital one million; another was "for encouraging the breed of horses in England, and improving of glebe and church lands, and repairing and rebuilding parsonage and vicarage houses." Why the clergy, who were so mainly interested in the latter clause, should have taken so much interest in the first, is only to be explained on the supposition that the scheme was projected by a knot of the fox-hunting parsons, once so common in England. The shares of this company were rapidly subscribed for. But the most absurd and preposterous of all, and which showed, more completely than any other, the utter madness of the people, was one started by an unknown adventurer, entitled, *A company for carrying on an undertaking of great advantage, but nobody to know what it is.* Were not the fact stated by scores of credible witnesses, it would be impossible to believe that any person could have been duped by such a project. The man of genius who essayed this bold and successful inroad upon public credulity, merely stated in his prospectus that the required capital was half a million, in five thousand shares of £100 each, deposit £2 per share. Each subscriber, paying his deposit, would be entitled to £100 per annum per share. How this immense profit was to be obtained, he did not condescend to inform them at that time, but promised that in a month full particulars should be duly announced, and a call made for the remaining £98 of the subscription. Next morning, at nine o'clock, this great man opened an office in Cornhill. Crowds of people beset his door, and when he shut up, at three o'clock, he found that no less than one thousand shares had been subscribed for, and the deposits paid. He was thus, in five hours, the winner of £2,000. He was philosopher enough to be contented with his venture, and set off the same evening for the Continent. He was never heard of again.

Well might Swift exclaim, comparing Change Alley to a gulf in the South Sea:

> *Subscribers here by thousands float,*
> *And jostle one another down,*
> *Each paddling in his leaky boat,*
> *And here they fish for gold and drown.*
>
> *Now buried in the depths below,*
> *Now mounted up to heaven again,*
> *They reel and stagger to and fro,*
> *At their wits' end, like drunken men.*
>
> *Meantime, secure on Garraway cliffs,*
> *A savage race, by shipwrecks fed.*
> *Lie waiting for the foundered skiffs.*
> *And strip the bodies of the dead.*

Another fraud that was very successful was that of the *Globe Permits*, as they were called. They were nothing more than square pieces of playing-cards, on which was the impression of a seal, in wax, bearing the sign of the Globe Tavern, in the neighborhood of Exchange Alley, with the inscription of *Sail-Cloth Permits*. The possessors enjoyed no other advantage from them than permission to subscribe at some future time to a new sail-cloth manufactory, projected by one who was then known to be a man of fortune, but who was afterward involved in the peculation and punishment of the South Sea directors. These permits sold for as much as sixty guineas in the Alley.

Persons of distinction, of both sexes, were deeply engaged in all these bubbles; those of the male sex going to taverns and coffee-houses to meet their brokers, and the ladies resorting for the same purpose to the shops of milliners and haberdashers. But it did not follow that all these people believed in the feasibility of the schemes to which they subscribed; it was enough for their purpose that their shares would, by stock-jobbing arts, be soon raised to a premium, when they got rid of them with all expedition to the really credulous. So great was the confusion of the crowd in the Alley, that shares in the same bubble were known to have been sold at the same instant ten percent, higher at one end of the Alley than at the other. Sensible men beheld the extraordinary infatuation of the people with sorrow and alarm. There were some both in and out of parliament who foresaw clearly the ruin that was impending. Mr. Walpole did not cease his gloomy forebodings. His fears were shared by all the thinking few, and impressed most forcibly upon the government. On the 11th of June, the day the parliament rose, the king published a proclamation, declaring that all these unlawful projects should be deemed public nuisances, and prosecuted accordingly, and forbidding any broker, under a penalty of five hundred pounds, from buying or selling any shares in them. Notwithstanding this proclamation, roguish speculators still carried them on, and the deluded people still encouraged them. On the 12th of July, an order of the Lords Justices assembled in privy council was published, dismissing all the petitions that had been presented for patents and charters, and dissolving all the bubble companies. The following copy of their lordships' order, containing a list of all these nefarious projects, will not be deemed uninteresting at the present time, when, at periodic intervals, there is but too much tendency in the public mind to indulge in similar practices:

At the Council Chamber, Whitehall, the 12th day of July, 1720. Present, their Excellencies the Lords Justices in Council.

Their Excellencies the Lords Justices, in council, taking into consideration the many inconveniences arising to the public from several projects set on foot for raising of joint-stock for various purposes, and that a great many of his majesty's subjects have been drawn in to part with their money on pretence of assurances that their petitions for patents and charters to enable them to carry on the same would be granted: to prevent such impositions, their excellencies this day ordered the said several petitions, together with such reports from the Board of Trade, and from his majesty's attorney and solicitor-general, as had been obtained thereon, to be laid before them; and after mature consideration thereof, were pleased, by advice of his majesty's privy council, to order that the said petitions be dismissed, which are as follow:

1. Petition of several persons, praying letters patent for carrying on a fishing trade by the name of the Grand Fishery of Great Britain.

2. Petition of the Company of the Royal Fishery of England, praying letters patent for such further powers as will effectually contribute to carry on the said fishery.

3. Petition of George James, on behalf of himself and divers persons of distinction concerned in a national fishery, praying letters patent of incorporation, to enable them to carry on the same.

4. Petition of several merchants, traders, and others, whose names are thereunto subscribed, praying to be incorporated for reviving and carrying on a whale fishery to Greenland and elsewhere.

5. Petition of Sir John Lambert and others thereto subscribing, on behalf of themselves and a great number of merchants, praying to be incorporated for carrying on a Greenland trade, and particularly a whale fishery in Davis's Straits.

6. Another petition for a Greenland trade.

7. Petition of several merchants, gentlemen, and citizens, praying to be incorporated for buying and building of ships to let or freight.

8. Petition of Samuel Antrim and others, praying for letters patent for sowing hemp and flax.

9. Petition of several merchants, masters of ships, sail-makers, and manufacturers of sail-cloth, praying a charter of incorporation, to enable them to carry on and promote the said manufactory by a joint-stock.

10. Petition of Thomas Boyd and several hundred merchants, owners and masters of ships, sail-makers, weavers, and other traders, praying a charter of incorporation, empowering them to borrow money for purchasing lands, in order to the manufacturing sail-cloth and fine holland.

11. Petition on behalf of several persons interested in a patent granted by the late King William and Queen Mary for the making of linen and sail-cloth, praying that no charter may be granted to any persons whatsoever for making sail-cloth but that the privilege now enjoyed by them may be confirmed, and likewise an additional power to carry on the cotton and cotton-silk manufactures.

12. Petition of several citizens, merchants and traders in London, and others, subscribers to a British stock for a general insurance from fire in any part of England, praying to be incorporated for carrying on the said undertaking.

13. Petition of several of his majesty's loyal subjects of the city of London and other parts of Great Britain, praying to be incorporated for carrying on a general insurance from losses by fire within the kingdom of England.

14. Petition of Thomas Burges and others his majesty's subjects thereto subscribing, in behalf of themselves and others, subscribers to a fund of £1,200,000 for carrying on a trade to his majesty's German dominions, praying to be incorporated

by the name of the Harburg Company.

15. Petition of Edward Jones, a dealer in timber, on behalf of himself and others, praying to be incorporated for the importation of timber from Germany.

16. Petition of several merchants of London, praying a charter of incorporation for carrying on a salt-work.

17. Petition of Captain Macphedris, of London, merchant, on behalf of himself and several merchants, clothiers, hatters, dyers and other traders, praying a charter of incorporation empowering them to raise a sufficient sum of money to purchase lands for planting and rearing a wood called madder, for the use of dyers.

18. Petition of Joseph Galendo, of London, snuff-maker, praying a patent for his invention to prepare and cure Virginia tobacco for snuff in Virginia, and making it into the same in all his majesty's dominions.

List of Bubbles

The following Bubble-Companies were by the same order declared to be illegal, and abolished accordingly:

1. For the importation of Swedish iron.
2. For supplying London with sea-coal. Capital, three millions.
3. For building and rebuilding houses throughout all England. Capital, three millions.
4. For making of muslin.
5. For carrying on and improving the British alum-works.
6. For effectually settling the island of Blanco and Sal Tartagus.
7. For supplying the town of Deal with fresh water.
8. For the importation of Flanders lace.

9. For improvement of lands in Great Britain. Capital, four millions.

10. For encouraging the breed of horses in England, and improving of glebe and church lands, and for repairing and rebuilding parsonage and vicarage houses.

11. For making of iron and steel in Great Britain.

12. For improving the land in the county of Flint. Capital, one million.

13. For purchasing lands to build on. Capital, two millions.

14. For trading in hair.

15. For erecting salt-works in Holy Island. Capital, two millions.

16. For buying and selling estates, and lending money on mortgage.

17. For carrying on an undertaking of great advantage, but nobody to know what it is.

18. For paving the streets of London. Capital, two millions.

19. For furnishing funerals to any part of Great Britain.

20. For buying and selling lands and lending money at interest. Capital five millions.

21. For carrying on the royal fishery of Great Britain. Capital ten millions.

22. For assuring of seamen's wages.

23. For erecting loan offices for the assistance and encouragement of the industrious. Capital, two millions.

24. For purchasing and improving leasable lands. Capital, four millions.

25. For importing pitch and tar, and other naval stores, from North Britain and America.

26. For the clothing, felt and pantile trade.

27. For purchasing and improving a manor and royalty in Essex.

28. For insuring of horses. Capital, two millions.

29. For exporting the woollen manufacture, and importing copper, brass, and iron. Capital, four millions.

30. For a grand dispensary. Capital, three millions.

31. For erecting mills and purchasing lead-mines. Capital, two millions.

32. For improving the art of making soap.

33. For a settlement on the island of Santa Cruz.

34. For sinking pits and smelting lead ore in Derbyshire.

35. For making glass bottles and other glass.

36. For a wheel for perpetual motion. Capital, one million.

37. For improving of gardens.

38. For insuring and increasing children's fortunes.

39. For entering and loading goods at the Custom-house, and for negotiating business for merchants.

40. For carrying on a woollen manufacture in the north of England.

41. For importing walnut-trees from Virginia. Capital, two millions.

42. For making Manchester stuffs of thread and cotton.

43. For making Joppa and Castile soap.

44. For improving the wrought-iron and steel manufactures of this kingdom. Capital, four millions.

45. For dealing in lace, hollands, cambrics, lawns, etc. Capital, two millions.

46. For trading in and improving certain commodities of the produce of this kingdom, etc. Capital, three millions.

47. For supplying the London markets with cattle.

48. For making looking-glasses, coach-glasses, etc. Capital, two millions.

49. For working the tin and lead mines in Cornwall and Derbyshire.

50. For making rape-oil.

51. For importing beaver fur. Capital, two millions.

52. For making pasteboard and packing-paper.

53. For importing of oils and other materials used in the woollen manufacture.

54. For improving and increasing the silk manufactures.

55. For lending money on stock, annuities, tallies, etc.

56. For paying pensions to widows and others, at a small discount. Capital, two millions. 57. For improving malt liquors. Capital, four millions.

58. For a grand American fishery.

59. For purchasing and improving the fenny lands in Lincolnshire. Capital, two millions. 60. For improving the paper manufacture of Great Britain.

61. The Bottomry Company.

62. For drying malt by hot air.

63. For carrying on a trade in the river Oro nooko.

64. For the more effectual making of baize, in Colchester and other parts of Great Britain.

65. For buying of naval stores, supplying the victualling, and paying the wages of the workmen.

66. For employing poor artificers, and furnishing merchants and others with watches.

67. For improvement of tillage and the breed of cattle.

68. Another for the improvement of our breed in horses.

69. Another for a horse-insurance.

70. For carrying on the corn trade of Great Britain.

71. For insuring to all masters and mistresses the losses they may sustain by servants. Capital, three millions.

72. For erecting houses or hospitals for taking in and maintaining illegitimate children. Capital, two millions.

73. For bleaching coarse sugars, without the use of fire or loss of substance.

74. For building turnpikes and wharfs in Great Britain.

75. For insuring from thefts and robberies.

76. For extracting silver from lead.

77. For making china and delf ware. Capital, one million.

78. For importing tobacco, and exporting it again to Sweden and the north of Europe. Capital, four millions.

79. For making iron with pit coal.

80. For furnishing the cities of London and Westminster with hay and straw. Capital, three millions.

81. For a sail and packing-cloth manufactory in Ireland.

82. For taking up ballast.

83. For buying and fitting out ships to suppress pirates.

84. For the importation of timber from Wales. Capital, two millions.

85. For rock-salt.

86. For the transmutation of quicksilver into a malleable fine metal.

Besides these bubbles, many others sprang up daily, in spite of the condemnation of the government and the ridicule of the still sane portion, of the public. The print-shops teemed with caricatures, and the newspapers with epigrams and satires, upon the prevalent folly. An ingenious cardmaker published a pack of South Sea playing cards, which are now extremely rare, each card containing, besides the usual figures of a very small size, in. one corner, a caricature of a bubble company, with appropriate verses underneath. One of the most famous bubbles was *Puckle's Machine Company*, for discharging round and square cannon-balls and bullets, and making a total revolution in the art of war. Its pretensions to public favor were thus summed up on the eight of spades:

> *A rare intention to destroy the crowd*
> *Of fools at home instead of fools abroad.*

Fear not, my friends, this terrible machine,
They're only wounded who have shares therein.

The nine of hearts was a caricature of the English Copper and Brass Company, with the following epigram:

The headlong fool that wants to be a swopper
Of gold and silver coin for English copper,
May, in Change Alley, prove himself an ass,
And give rich metal for adultrate brass.

The eight of diamonds celebrated the company for the colonization of Acadia, with this doggerel:

He that is rich, and wants to fool away
A good round sum in North America,
Let him subscribe himself a headlong sharer.
And asses' ears shall honor him or bearer.

And in a similar style every card of the pack exposed some knavish scheme, and ridiculed the persons who were its dupes. It was computed that the total amount of the sums proposed for carrying on these projects was upwards of three hundred millions sterling.

It is time, however, to return to the great South Sea gulf that swallowed the fortunes of so many thousands of the avaricious and the credulous. On the 29th of May, the stock had risen as high as five hundred, and about two-thirds of the government annuitants had exchanged the securities of the state for those of the South Sea Company. During the whole of the month of May the stock continued to rise, and on the 28th it was quoted at five hundred and fifty. In four days after this, it took a prodigious leap, rising suddenly from five hundred and fifty to eight hundred and ninety. It was now the general opinion that the stock could rise no higher, and many persons took that opportunity of selling out, with a view of realizing their profits. Many noblemen and persons in the train of the king, and about to accompany him to Hanover, were also anxious to sell out. So many sellers, and so few buyers, appeared in the Alley on the 3rd of June, that the stock fell at once from eight hundred and ninety to six hundred and forty. The directors were alarmed, and gave their agents orders to buy. Their efforts succeeded. Toward evening, confidence was restored, and the stock advanced to seven hundred and fifty. It continued at this price, with some slight fluctuation, until the company closed their books on the 22nd of June. It would be needless and uninteresting to detail the various arts employed by the directors to keep up the price of stock. It will be sufficient to state that it finally rose to one thousand percent. It was quoted at this price in the commencement of August. The bubble was then full-blown, and began to quiver and shake preparatory to its bursting.—(Note 2.)

Many of the government annuitants expressed dissatisfaction against the directors. They accused them of partiality in making out the lists for shares in each subscription. Further uneasiness was occasioned by its being generally known that Sir John Blunt, the chairman, and some others, had sold out. During the whole of the month of August the stock fell, and on the 2nd of September it was quoted at seven hundred only.

The state of things now became alarming. To prevent, if possible, the utter extinction of public confidence in their proceedings, the directors summoned a general court of the whole corporation, to meet in Merchant Tailors' Hall on the 8th of September. By nine o'clock in the morning, the room was filled to suffocation; Cheapside was blocked up by a crowd unable to gain admittance, and the greatest excitement prevailed. The directors and their friends mustered in great numbers. Sir John Fellowes, the sub-governor, was called to the chair. He acquainted the assembly with the cause of their meeting; read to them the several resolutions of the court of directors, and gave them an account of their proceedings; of the taking in the redeemable and unredeemable funds, and of the subscriptions in money. Mr. Secretary Craggs then made a short speech, wherein he commended the conduct of the directors, and urged that nothing could more effectually contribute to the bringing this scheme to perfection than union among themselves. He concluded with a motion for thanking the court of directors for their prudent and skillful management, and for desiring them to proceed in such manner as they should think most proper for the interest and advantage of the corporation. Mr. Hungerford, who had rendered himself very conspicuous in the House of Commons for his zeal on behalf of the South Sea Company, and who was shrewdly suspected to have been a considerable gainer by knowing the right time to sell out, was very magniloquent on this occasion. He said that he had seen the rise and fall, the decay and resurrection of many communities of this nature, but that, in his opinion, none had ever performed such wonderful things in so short a time as the South Sea Company. They had done more than the crown, the pulpit, or the bench could do. They had reconciled all parties in one common interest; they had laid asleep, if not wholly extinguished, all the domestic jars and animosities of the nation. By the rise of their stock, moneyed men had vastly increased their fortunes; country gentlemen had seen the value of their lands doubled and trebled in their hands. They had at the same time done good to the church, not a few of the reverend clergy having got great sums by the project. In short, they had enriched the whole nation, and he hoped they had not forgotten themselves. There was some hissing at the latter part of this speech, which, for the extravagance of its eulogy, was not far removed from satire; but the directors and their friends, and all the winners in the room, applauded vehemently. The Duke of Portland spoke in a similar strain, and expressed his great wonder why anybody should be dissatisfied; of course, he was a winner by his speculations, and in a condition similar to that of the fat alderman in *Joe Miller's Jests*, who, whenever he had eaten a good dinner, folded his hands upon his paunch, and expressed his doubts whether there could be a hungry man in the world.

Several resolutions were passed at this meeting, but they had no effect upon the public. Upon the very same evening the stock fell to six hundred and forty, and on the morrow to five hundred and forty. Day after day it continued to fall, until it was as low as four hundred. In a letter, dated September 13th, from Mr. Broderick, M.P., to Lord Chancellor Middleton, and published in Coxe's *Walpole*, the former says: "Various are the conjectures why the South Sea directors have suffered the cloud to break so early. I made no doubt but they would do so when they found it to their advantage. They have stretched credit so far beyond what it would bear, that specie proves insufficient to support it. Their most considerable men have drawn out, securing themselves by the losses of the deluded, thoughtless numbers, whose understandings have been overruled by avarice and the hope of making mountains out of molehills. Thousands of families will be reduced to beggary. The consternation is inexpressible—the rage beyond description, and the case altogether so desperate, that I do not see any plan or scheme so much as thought of for averting the blow; so that I cannot pretend to guess what is next to be done." Ten days afterward, the stock still falling, he writes: "The company have yet come to no determination, for they are in such a wood that they know not which way to turn. By several gentlemen lately

CHAPTER XIII 213

come to town, I perceive the very name of a South Sea-man grows abominable in every country. A great many goldsmiths are already run off, and more will, daily. I question whether one-third, nay, one-fourth of them can stand it. From the very beginning, I founded my judgment of the whole affair upon the unquestionable maxim, that ten millions (which is more than our running cash) could not circulate two hundred millions beyond which our paper credit extended. That, therefore, whenever that should become doubtful, be the cause what it would, our noble state-machine must inevitably fall to the ground."

On the 12th of September, at the earnest solicitation of Mr. Secretary Craggs, several conferences were held between the directors of the South Sea and the directors of the Bank. A report which was circulated, that the latter had agreed to circulate six millions of the South Sea Company's bonds, caused the stock to rise to six hundred and seventy; but in the afternoon, as soon as the report was known to be groundless, the stock fell again to five hundred and eighty; the next day to five hundred and seventy, and so gradually to four hundred.[3]

The ministry were seriously alarmed at the aspect of affairs. The directors could not appear in the streets without being insulted; dangerous riots were every moment apprehended.

---

3. Gay (the poet), in that disastrous year, had a present from young Craggs of some South Sea stock, and once supposed himself to be master of twenty thousand pounds. His friends persuaded him to sell his share, but he dreamed of dignity and splendor, and could not bear to obstruct his own fortune. He was then importuned to sell as much as would purchase a hundred a year for life, "which," says Fenton, "will make you sure of a clean shirt and a shoulder of mutton every day." This counsel was rejected; the profit and principal were lost, and Gay sunk under the calamity so low that his life became in danger.—*Johnson's Lives of the Poets.*

Dispatches were sent off to the king at Hanover, praying his immediate return. Mr. Walpole, who was staying at his country seat, was sent for, that he might employ his known influence with the directors of the Bank of England to induce them to accept the proposal made by the South Sea Company for circulating a number of their bonds.

The Bank was very unwilling to mix itself up with the affairs of the company; it dreaded being involved in calamities which it could not relieve, and received all overtures with visible reluctance. But the universal voice of the nation called upon it to come to the rescue. Every person of note in commercial politics was called in to advise in the emergency. A rough draft of a contract drawn up by Mr. Walpole was ultimately adopted as the basis of further negotiations, and the public alarm abated a little.

On the following day, the 20th of September, a general court of the South Sea Company was held at Merchant Tailors' Hall, in which resolutions were carried, empowering the directors to agree with the Bank of England, or any other persons, to circulate the company's bonds, or make any other agreement with the Bank which they should think proper. One of the speakers, a Mr. Pulteney, said it was most surprising to see the extraordinary panic which had seized upon the people. Men were running to and fro in alarm and terror, their imaginations filled with some great calamity, the form and dimensions of which nobody knew:

*Black it stood as night —
Fierce as ten furies—terrible as hell.*

At a general court of the Bank of England, held two days afterward, the governor informed them of the several meetings that had been held on the affairs of the South Sea Company, adding that the directors had not yet thought fit to come to any decision upon the matter. A resolution was then proposed, and carried without a dissentient voice, empowering the directors to agree with those of the South Sea to circulate their bonds, to what sum, and upon what terms, and for what time, they might think proper.

Thus both parties were at liberty to act as they might judge best for the public interest. Books were opened at the Bank for subscription of three millions for the support of public credit, on the usual terms of £15 per cent deposit, £3 per cent premium, and £5 per cent interest. So great was the concourse of people in the early part of the morning, all eagerly bringing their money, that it was thought the subscription would be filled that day; but before noon the tide turned. In spite of all that could be done to prevent it, the South Sea company's stock fell rapidly. Their bonds were in such discredit, that a run commenced upon the most eminent goldsmiths and bankers, some of whom, having lent out great sums upon South Sea stock, were obliged to shut up their shops and abscond. The Sword-blade company, who had hitherto been the chief cashers of the South Sea Company, stopped payment. This being looked upon as but the beginning of evil, occasioned a great run upon the Bank, who were now obliged to pay out money much faster than they had received it upon the subscription in the morning. The day succeeding was a holiday (the 29th of September), and the Bank had a little breathing time. They bore up against the storm; but their former rivals, the South Sea Company, were wrecked upon it. Their stock fell to one hundred and fifty, and gradually, after various fluctuations, to one hundred and thirty-five.

The Bank, finding they were not able to restore public confidence, and stem the tide of ruin, without running the risk of being swept away with those they intended to save, declined to carry out the agreement into which they had partially entered. They were under no obligation whatever to continue; for the so-called Bank contract was nothing more than the rough draft of an agreement, in which blanks had been left for several important particulars, and which contained no penalty for their secession. "And thus," to use the words of the Parliamentary History, "were seen, in the space of eight months, the rise, progress, and fall of that mighty fabric, which being wound up by mysterious springs to a wonderful height had fixed the eyes and expectations of all Europe, but whose foundation, being fraud, illusion, credulity, and infatuation, fell to the ground as soon as the artful management of its directors was discovered."

In the hey-day of its blood, during the progress of this dangerous delusion, the manners of the nation became sensibly corrupted. The parliamentary inquiry, set on foot to discover the delinquents, disclosed scenes of infamy, disgraceful alike to the morals of the offenders and the intellects of the people among whom they had arisen. It is a deeply interesting study to investigate all the evils that were the result. Nations, like individuals, cannot become desperate gamblers with impunity. Punishment is sure to overtake them sooner or later. A celebrated writer is quite wrong when he says "that such an era as this is the most unfavorable for a historian; that no reader of sentiment and imagination can be entertained or interested by a detail of transactions such as these, which admit of no warmth, no coloring, no embellishment; a detail of which only serves to exhibit an inanimate picture of tasteless vice and mean degeneracy." On the contrary—and Smollett might have discovered it, if he had been in the humor—the subject is capable of inspiring as much interest as even a novelist can desire. Is there no warmth in the despair of a plundered people?—no life and animation in the picture which might be drawn of the woes of hundreds of impoverished and ruined families? of the wealthy of yesterday become the beggars of today? of the powerful and influential changed into exiles and outcasts, and the voice of self-reproach and imprecation resounding from every corner of the land? Is it a dull or uninstructive picture to see a whole people shaking suddenly off the trammels of reason, and running wild after a golden vision, refusing obstinately to believe that it is not real, till, like a deluded hind running after an *ignis fatuus*, they are plunged into a quagmire? But in this false spirit has history too often been written. The intrigues of unworthy courtiers to gain the favor of still more unworthy kings, or the records of murderous battles and sieges, have been dilated on, and told over and over again, with all the eloquence of style and all the charms of fancy; while the circumstances which have most deeply affected the morals and welfare of the people have been passed over with but slight notice, as dry and dull, and capable of neither warmth nor coloring.

During the progress of this famous bubble, England presented a singular spectacle. The public mind was in a state of unwholesome fermentation. Men were no longer satisfied with the slow but sure profits of cautious industry. The hope of boundless wealth for the morrow made them heedless and extravagant for today. A luxury, till then unheard of, was introduced, bringing in its train a corresponding laxity of morals. The overbearing insolence of ignorant men, who had arisen to sudden wealth by successful gambling, made men of true gentility of mind and manners blush that gold should have power to raise the unworthy in the scale of society. The haughtiness of some of these "cyphering cits," as they were termed by Sir Richard Steele, was remembered against them in the day of their adversity. In the parliamentary inquiry, many of the directors suffered more for their insolence than for their peculation. One of them, who, in the full-blown pride of an ignorant rich man, had said that he would feed his horse upon gold, was reduced almost to bread and water for himself; every haughty look, every overbearing speech, was set down, and repaid them a hundred fold in poverty and humiliation.— (Notes 3, 4.)

The state of matters all over the country was so alarming, that George I shortened his intended stay in Hanover, and returned in all haste to England. He arrived on the 11th of November, and parliament was summoned to meet on the 8th of December. In the meantime, public meetings were held in every considerable town of the empire, at which petitions were adopted, praying the vengeance of the legislature upon the South Sea directors, who, by their fraudulent practices, had brought the nation to the brink of ruin. Nobody seemed to imagine that the nation itself was as culpable as the South Sea Company. Nobody blamed the credulity and avarice of the people—the degrading lust of gain, which had swallowed up every nobler quality in the national character, or the infatuation which had made the multitude run their heads with such frantic eagerness into the net held out for them by scheming projectors. These things were never mentioned. The people were a simple, honest, hard-working people, ruined by a gang of robbers, who were to be hanged, drawn, and quartered without mercy.

This was the almost unanimous feeling of the country. The two houses of parliament were not more reasonable. Before the guilt of the South Sea directors was known, punishment was the only cry. The king, in his speech from the throne, expressed his hope that they would remember that all their prudence, temper, and resolution, were necessary to find out and apply the proper remedy for their misfortunes. In the debate on the answer to the address, several speakers indulged in the most violent invectives against the directors of the South Sea project. The Lord Molesworth was particularly vehement:

"It had been said by some, that there was no law to punish

the directors of the South Sea Company, who were justly looked upon as the authors of the present misfortunes of the state. In his opinion, they ought upon this occasion to follow the example of the ancient Romans, who, having no law against parricide, because their legislators supposed no son could be so unnaturally wicked as to imbrue his hands in his father's blood, made a law to punish this heinous crime as soon as it was committed. They adjudged the guilty wretch to be sewn in a sack, and thrown alive into the Tiber. He looked upon the contrivers and executors of the villainous South Sea scheme as the parricides of their country, and should be satisfied to see them tied in like manner in sacks, and thrown into the Thames." Other members spoke with as much want of temper and discretion. Mr. Walpole was more moderate. He recommended that their first care should be to restore public credit. "If the city of London were on fire, all wise men would aid in extinguishing the flames, and preventing the spread of the conflagration, before they inquired after the incendiaries. Public credit had received a dangerous wound, and lay bleeding, and they ought to apply a speedy remedy to it. It was time enough to punish the assassin afterward." On the 9th of December, an address, in answer to his majesty's speech, was agreed upon, after an amendment, which was carried without a division, that words should be added expressive of the determination of the House not only to seek a remedy for the national distresses, but to punish the authors of them.

The inquiry proceeded rapidly. The directors were ordered to lay before the House a full account of all their proceedings. Resolutions were passed to the effect that the calamity was mainly owing to the vile arts of stock-jobbers, and that nothing could tend more to the reestablishment of public credit than a law to prevent this infamous practice. Mr. Walpole then rose, and said, that "as he had previously hinted, he had spent some time upon a scheme for restoring public credit, but that the execution of it depending upon a position which had been laid down as fundamental, he thought it proper, before he opened out his scheme, to be informed whether he might rely upon that foundation. It was, whether the subscription of public debts and encumbrances, money subscriptions, and other contracts, made with the South Sea Company, should remain in the present state?" This question occasioned an animated debate. It was finally agreed, by a majority of 259 against 117, that all these contracts should remain in their present state, unless altered for the relief of the proprietors by a general court of the South Sea Company, or set aside by due course of law. On the following day, Mr. Walpole laid before a committee of the whole House his scheme for the restoration of public credit, which was, in substance, to engraft nine millions of South Sea stock into the Bank of England, and the same sum into the East India Company upon certain conditions. The plan was favorably received by the House. After some few objections, it was ordered that proposals should be received from the two great corporations. They were both unwilling to lend their aid, and the plan met with a warm but fruitless opposition at the general courts summoned for the purpose of deliberating upon it. They, however, ultimately agreed upon the terms on which they would consent to circulate the South Sea bonds, and their report being presented to the committee, a bill was brought in under the superintendence of Mr. Walpole, and safely carried through both Houses of Parliament.

A bill was at the same time brought in for restraining the South Sea directors, governor, sub governor, treasurer, cashier, and clerks from leaving the kingdom for a year, and for discovering their estates and effects, and preventing them from transporting or alienating the same. All the most influential members of the House supported the bill. Mr. Shippen, seeing

CHAPTER XIII 221

Mr. Secretary Craggs in his place, and believing the injurious rumors that were afloat of that minister's conduct in the South Sea business, determined to touch him to the quick. He said he was glad to see a British House of Commons resuming its pristine vigor and spirit, and acting with so much unanimity for the public good. It was necessary to secure the persons and estates of the South Sea directors and their officers; "but," he added, looking fixedly at Mr. Craggs as he spoke, "there were other men in high station, whom, in time, he would not be afraid to name, who were no less guilty than the directors." Mr. Craggs arose in great wrath, and said, that if the innuendo were directed against him, he was ready to give satisfaction to any man who questioned him, either in the House or out of it. Loud cries of order immediately arose on every side. In the midst of the uproar, Lord Molesworth got up, and expressed his wonder at the boldness of Mr. Craggs in challenging the whole House of Commons. He, Lord Molesworth, though somewhat old, past sixty, would answer Mr. Craggs whatever he had to say in the House, and he trusted there were plenty of young men beside him, who would not be afraid to look Mr. Craggs in the face out of the House. The cries of order again resounded from every side; the members arose simultaneously; everybody seemed to be vociferating at once. The Speaker in vain called order. The confusion lasted several minutes, during which Lord Molesworth and Mr. Craggs were almost the only members who kept their seats. At last, the call for Mr. Craggs became so violent, that he thought proper to submit to the universal feeling of the House, and explain his unparliamentary expression. He said, that by giving satisfaction to the impugners of his conduct in that House, he did not mean that he would fight, but that he would explain his conduct. Here the matter ended, and the House proceeded to debate in what manner they should conduct their inquiry into the affairs of the South

Sea Company, whether in a grand or a select committee. Ultimately, a secret committee of thirteen was appointed, with power to send for persons, papers, and records.

The Lords were as zealous and as hasty as the Commons. The Bishop of Rochester said the scheme had been like a pestilence. The Duke of Wharton said the House ought to show no respect of persons; that, for his part, he would give up the dearest friend he had, if he had been engaged in the project. The nation had been plundered in a most shameful and flagrant manner, and he would go as far as anybody in the punishment of the offenders. Lord Stanhope said, that every farthing possessed by the criminals, whether directors or not directors, ought to be confiscated, to make good the public losses.

During all this time the public excitement was extreme. We learn from Cox's *Walpole*, that the very name of a South Sea director was thought to be synonymous with every species of fraud and villainy. Petitions from counties, cities, and boroughs, in all parts of the kingdom, were presented, crying for the justice due to an injured nation and the punishment of the villainous peculators. Those moderate men, who would not go to extreme lengths, even in the punishment of the guilty, were accused of being accomplices, were exposed to repeated insults and virulent invectives, and devoted, both in anonymous letters and public writings, to the speedy vengeance of an injured people. The accusations against Mr. Aislabie, Chancellor of the Exchequer, and Mr. Craggs another member of the ministry, were so loud, that the House of Lords resolved to proceed at once into the investigation concerning them. It was ordered, on the 21st of January, that all brokers concerned in the South Sea scheme should lay before the House an account of the stock or subscriptions bought or sold by them for any of the officers of the Treasury or Exchequer, or in trust for any of them, since

Michaelmas, 1719. When this account was delivered, it appeared that large quantities of stock had been transferred to the use of Mr. Aislabie. Five of the South Sea directors, including Mr. Edward Gibbon, the grandfather of the celebrated historian, were ordered into the custody of the black rod. Upon a motion made by Earl Stanhope, it was unanimously resolved, that the taking in or giving credit for stock without a valuable consideration actually paid or sufficiently secured, or the purchasing stock by any director or agent of the South Sea Company for the use or benefit of any member of the administration, or any member of either house of parliament, during such time as the South Sea bill was yet pending in parliament, was a notorious and dangerous corruption. Another resolution was passed a few days afterward, to the effect that several of the directors and officers of the company having, in a clandestine manner, sold their own stock to the company, had been guilty of a notorious fraud and breach of trust, and had thereby mainly caused the unhappy turn of affairs that had so much affected public credit. Mr. Aislabie resigned his office as Chancellor of the Exchequer, and absented himself from parliament, until the formal inquiry into his individual guilt was brought under the consideration of the legislature.

In the meantime, Knight, the treasurer of the company, and who was entrusted with all the dangerous secrets of the dishonest directors, packed up his books and documents and made his escape from the country. He embarked in disguise, in a small boat on the river, and proceeding to a vessel hired for the purpose, was safely conveyed to Calais. The Committee of Secrecy informed the House of the circumstance, when it was resolved unanimously that two addresses should be presented to the king; the first praying that he would issue a proclamation offering a reward for the apprehension of Knight; and the second, that he would give immediate orders to stop the ports, and to take effectual care of the coasts, to prevent the said Knight, or any other officers of the South Sea Company, from escaping out of the kingdom. The ink was hardly dry upon these addresses before they were carried to the king by Mr. Methuen, deputed by the House for that purpose. The same evening a royal proclamation was issued, offering a reward of two thousand pounds for the apprehension of Knight. The Commons ordered the doors of the house to be locked and the keys to be placed on the table. General Ross, one of the members of the Committee of Secrecy, acquainted them that they had already discovered a train of the deepest villainy and fraud that hell had ever contrived to ruin a nation, which in due time they would lay before the House. In the meantime, in order to a further discovery, the committee thought it highly necessary to secure the persons of some of the directors and principal South Sea officers, and to seize their papers. A motion to this effect having been made was carried unanimously. Sir Robert Chaplin, Sir Theodore Janssen, Mr. Sawbridge, and Mr. F. Eyles, members of the House, and directors of the South Sea Company, were summoned to appear in their places, and answer for their corrupt practices. Sir Theodore Janssen and Mr. Sawbridge answered to their names, and endeavored to exculpate themselves. The House heard them patiently, and then ordered them to withdraw. A motion was then made, and carried *nemine contradicente*, that they had been guilty of a notorious breach of trust—had occasioned much loss to great numbers of his majesty's subjects, and had highly prejudiced the public credit. It was then ordered that for their offence they should be expelled the House and taken into the custody of the sergeant-at-arms. Sir Robert Chaplin and Mr. Eyles, attending in their places four days afterward, were also expelled the House. It was resolved at the same time to address the king to give directions to his ministers at foreign courts to make application for Knight, that he might be delivered up to the English authorities, in case he took refuge in any of their dominions. The king at once agreed, and messengers were dispatched to all parts of the continent the same night.

Among the directors taken into custody was Sir John Blunt, the man whom popular opinion has generally accused of having been the original author and father of the scheme. This man, we are informed by Pope, in his epistle to Allen Lord Bathurst, was a Dissenter, of a most religious deportment, and professed to be a great believer:

> *'God cannot love,' says Blunt, with tearless eyes,*
> *'The wretch he starves,' and piously denies. . . .*
> *Much-injur'd Blunt! why bears he Britain's hate?*
> *A wizard told him in these words our fate:*
> *'At length corruption, like a general flood,*
> *So long by watchful ministers withstood,*
> *Shall deluge all; and avarice, creeping on,*
> *Spread like a low-born mist, and blot the sun;*
> *Statesman and patriot ply alike the stocks,*
> *Peeress and butler share alike the box,*
> *And judges job, and bishops bite the town,*
> *And mighty dukes pack cards for half-a-crown:*
> *See Britain sunk in Lucre's sordid charms,*
> *And France revenged on Anne's and Edward's arms!*
> *'Twas no court-badge, great Scrivener! fir'd thy brain,*
> *Nor lordly luxury, nor city gain:*
> *No, 'twas thy righteous end, asham'd to see*
> *Senates degen'rate, patriots disagree,*
> *And nobly wishing party-rage to cease,*
> *To buy both sides, and give thy country peace.*
>
> —*Pope's Epistle to Allen Lord Bathurst.*

He constantly declaimed against the luxury and corruption of the age, the partiality of parliaments, and the misery of party-spirit. He was particularly eloquent against avarice in great and noble persons. He was originally a scrivener, and afterward became not only a director, but the most active manager of the South Sea Company. Whether it was during his career in this capacity that he first began to declaim against the avarice of the great, we are not informed. He certainly must have seen enough of it to justify his severest anathema; but if the preacher had himself been free from the vice he condemned, his declamations would have had a better effect. He was brought up in custody to the bar of the House of Lords, and underwent a long examination. He refused to answer several important questions. He said he had been examined already by a committee of the House of Commons, and as he did not remember his answers and might contradict himself, he refused to answer before another tribunal. This declaration, in itself an indirect proof of guilt, occasioned some commotion in the House. He was again asked peremptorily whether he had ever sold any portion of the stock to any member of the administration, or any member of either house of parliament, to facilitate the passing of the bill. He again declined to answer. He was anxious, he said, to treat the House with all possible respect, but he thought it hard to be compelled to accuse himself. After several ineffectual attempts to refresh his memory, he was directed to withdraw. A violent discussion ensued between the friends and opponents of the ministry. It was asserted that the administration were no strangers to the convenient taciturnity of Sir John Blunt. The Duke of Wharton made a reflection upon the Earl Stanhope, which the latter warmly resented. He spoke under great excitement, and with such vehemence as to cause a sudden determination of blood to the head. He felt himself so ill that he was obliged to leave the House and retire to his chamber. He was cupped immediately, and also let blood on the following morning, but with slight relief. The fatal result was not anticipated. Toward evening he became drowsy, and turning himself on his face, expired. The sudden death of this statesman caused great grief to the nation. George I was exceedingly affected, and shut himself up for some hours in his closet, inconsolable for his loss.—(Note 6.)

Knight, the treasurer of the company, was apprehended at Tirlemont, near Liege, by one of the secretaries of Mr. Leathes, the British resident at Brussels, and lodged in the citadel of Antwerp. Repeated applications were made to the court of Austria to deliver him up, but in vain. Knight threw himself upon the protection of the states of Brabant, and demanded to be tried in that country. It was a privilege granted to the states of Brabant by one of the articles of the Joyeuse Entrée, that every criminal apprehended in that country should be tried in that country. The states insisted on their privilege, and refused to deliver Knight to the British authorities. The latter did not cease their solicitations; but in the meantime Knight escaped from the citadel.

On the 16th of February, the Committee of Secrecy made their first report to the House. They stated that their inquiry had been attended with numerous difficulties and embarrassments; everyone they had examined had endeavored, as far as in him lay, to defeat the ends of justice. In some of the books produced before them, false and fictitious entries had been made; in others, there were entries of money with blanks for the name of the stockholders. There were frequent erasures and alterations, and in some of the books, leaves were torn out. They also found that some books of great importance had been destroyed altogether, and that some had been taken away or secreted. At the very entrance into their inquiry, they had observed that the matters referred to them were of great variety and extent. Many persons had been entrusted with various parts in the execution of the law, and under color thereof, had acted in an unwarrantable manner, in disposing of the properties of many thousands of persons, amounting to many millions of money. They discovered that, before the South Sea Act was passed, there was an entry in the company's books of the sum of £1,259,325, upon account of stock stated to have been sold to the amount of £574,500. This stock was all fictitious, and had been disposed of with a view to promote the passing of the bill. It was noted as sold on various days, and at various prices, from 150 to 325 percent. Being surprised to see so large an account disposed of at a time when the company were not empowered to increase their capital, the committee determined to investigate most carefully the whole transaction. The governor, sub-governor, and several directors were brought before them, and examined rigidly. They found that, at the time these entries were made, the company was not in possession of such a quantity of stock, having in their own right only a small quantity, not exceeding thirty thousand pounds at the utmost. Pursuing the inquiry, they found that this amount of stock was to be esteemed as taken in or holden by the company for the benefit of the pretended purchasers, although no mutual agreement was made for its delivery or acceptance at any certain time. No money was paid down, nor any deposit or security whatever given to the company by the supposed purchasers; so that if the stock had fallen, as might have been expected had the act not passed, they would have sustained no loss. If, on the contrary, the price of stock advanced (as it actually did, by the success of the scheme), the difference by the advanced price was to be made good to them. Accordingly, after the passing of the act, the account of stock was made up and adjusted with Mr. Knight, and the pretended purchasers were paid the difference out of the company's cash. This fictitious stock, which had been chiefly at the disposal of Sir John Blunt, Mr. Gibbon, and Mr. Knight, was distributed among several members of the government and their connections, by way of bribe, to facilitate the passing of the bill. To the Earl of Sunderland was assigned £50,000 of this stock; to the Duchess of Kendal, £10,000; to the Countess of Platen, £10,000; to her two nieces, £10,000; to Mr. Secretary Craggs, £30,000; to Mr. Charles Stanhope (one of the secretaries of the Treasury), £10,000; to the Sword-blade company, £50,000. It also appeared that Mr. Stanhope had received the enormous sum of £250,000 as the difference in the price of some stock, through the hands of Turner, Caswall and Co., but that his name had been partly erased from their books, and altered to Stangape. Aislabie, the Chancellor of the Exchequer, had made profits still more abominable. He had an account with the same firm, who were also South Sea directors, to the amount of £794,451. He had, besides, advised the company to make their second subscription one million and a half, instead of a million, by their own authority, and without any warrant. The third subscription had been conducted in a manner as disgraceful. Mr. Aislabie's name was down for £70,000; Mr. Craggs, senior, for £659,000; the Earl of Sunderland's for £160,000; and Mr. Stanhope for £47,000. This report was succeeded by six others, less important. At the end of the last, the committee declared that the absence of Knight, who had been principally entrusted, prevented them from carrying on their inquiries.

The first report was ordered to be printed, and taken into consideration on the next day but one, succeeding. After a very angry and animated debate, a series of resolutions were agreed to, condemnatory of the conduct of the directors, of the members of parliament, and of the administration concerned with them; and declaring that they ought, each and all, to make satisfaction out of their own estates for the injury they had done the public. Their practices were declared to be corrupt, infamous, and dangerous; and a bill was ordered to be brought in for the relief of the unhappy sufferers.

Mr. Charles Stanhope was the first person brought to account for his share in these transactions. He urged in his defence that, for some years past, he had lodged all the money he was possessed of in Mr. Knight's hands, and whatever stock Mr. Knight had taken in for him, he had paid a valuable consideration for it. As for the stock that had been bought for him by Turner, Caswall, and Co., he knew nothing about it. Whatever had been done in that matter was done without his authority, and he could not be responsible for it. Turner and Co. took the latter charge upon themselves; but it was notorious to every unbiased and unprincipled person that Mr. Stanhope was a gainer of the £250,000 which lay in the hands of that firm to his credit. He was, however, acquitted by a majority of three only. The greatest exertions were made to screen him. Lord Stanhope, the son of the Earl of Chesterfield, went round to the wavering members, using all the eloquence he was possessed of to induce them either to vote for the acquittal, or to absent themselves from the House. Many weak-headed, country gentlemen were led astray by his persuasions, and the result was as already stated. The acquittal caused the greatest discontent throughout the country. Mobs of a menacing character assembled in different parts of London; fears of riots were generally entertained, especially as the examination of a still greater delinquent was expected by many to have a similar termination. Mr. Aislabie, whose high office and deep responsibilities should have kept him honest, even had. native principle been insufficient, was very justly regarded as, perhaps, the greatest criminal of all. His case was entered into on the day succeeding the acquittal of Mr. Stanhope. Great excitement prevailed, and the lobbies and avenues of the House were beset by crowds impatient to know the result. The debate lasted the whole day. Mr. Aislabie found few friends: his guilt was so apparent and so heinous, that nobody had courage to stand up in his favor. It was finally resolved, without a dissentient voice, that Mr. Aislabie had encouraged and promoted the destructive execution of the South Sea scheme, with a view to his own exorbitant profit, and had combined with the directors in their pernicious practices, to the ruin of the public trade and credit of the kingdom: that he should, for his offences, be ignominiously expelled from the House of Commons, and committed a close prisoner to the Tower of London; that he should be restrained from going out of the kingdom for a whole year, or till the end of the next session of parliament; and that he should make out a correct account of all his estate, in order that it might be applied to the relief of those who had suffered by his malpractices.

This verdict caused the greatest joy. Though it was delivered at half-past twelve at night, it soon spread over the city. Several persons illuminated their houses in token of their joy. On the following day, when Mr. Aislabie was conveyed to the Tower, the mob assembled on Tower Hill with the intention of hooting and pelting him. Not succeeding in this, they kindled a large bonfire, and danced around it in the exuberance of their delight; Several bonfires were made in other places; London presented the appearance of a holiday, and people congratulated one another as if they had just escaped from some great calamity. The rage upon the acquittal of Mr. Stanhope had grown to such a height, that none could tell where it would have ended had Mr. Aislabie met with the like indulgence.

To increase the public satisfaction, Sir George Caswall, of the firm of Turner, Caswall & Co., was expelled from the House on the following day, committed to the Tower, and ordered to refund the sum of £250,000.

That part of the report of the Committee of Secrecy

which related to the Earl of Sunderland was next taken into consideration. Every effort was made to clear his lordship from the imputation. As the case against him rested chiefly on the evidence extorted from Sir John Blunt, great pains were taken to make it appear that Sir John's word was not to be believed, especially in a matter affecting the honor of a peer and privy councillor. All the friends of the ministry rallied around the earl, it being generally reported that a verdict of guilty against him would bring a Tory ministry into power. He was eventually acquitted by a majority of 233 against 172; but the country was convinced of his guilt. The greatest indignation was everywhere expressed, and menacing mobs again assembled in London. Happily, no disturbance took place.

This was the day on which Mr. Craggs the elder expired. The morrow had been appointed for the consideration of his case. It was very generally believed that he had poisoned himself. It appeared, however, that grief for the loss of his son, one of the secretaries of the Treasury, who had died five weeks previously of the smallpox, preyed much on his mind. For this son, dearly beloved, he had been amassing vast heaps of riches: he had been getting money, but not honestly; and he for whose sake he had bartered his honor and sullied his fame was now no more. The dread of further exposure increased his trouble of mind, and ultimately brought on an apoplectic fit, in which he expired. He left a fortune of a million and a half, which was afterward confiscated for the benefit of the sufferers by the unhappy delusion he had been so mainly instrumental in raising.

One by one the case of every director of the company was taken into consideration. A sum amounting to two millions and fourteen thousand pounds was confiscated from their estates towards repairing the mischief they had done, each man being allowed a certain residue in proportion to his conduct and circumstances, with which he might begin the world anew.

Sir John Blunt was only allowed £5,000 out of his fortune of upward of £183,000; Sir John Fellows was allowed £10,000 out of £243,000; Sir Theodore Janssen, £50,000 out of £243,000; Mr. Edward Gibbon, £10,000 out of £106,000; Sir John Lambert, £5,000 out of £72,000. Others, less deeply involved, were treated with greater liberality. Gibbon, the historian, whose grandfather was the Mr. Edward Gibbon so severely mulcted, has given, in the *Memoirs of his Life and Writings*, an interesting account of the proceedings in parliament at this time. He owns that he is not an unprejudiced witness; but, as all the writers from which it is possible to extract any notice of the proceedings of these disastrous years were prejudiced on the other side, the statements of the great historian become of additional value. If only on the principle of *audi alteram partem*, his opinion is entitled to consideration. "In the year 1716," he says, "my grandfather was elected one of the directors of the South Sea Company, and his books exhibited the proof that before his acceptance of that fatal office, he had acquired an independent fortune of £60,000. But his fortune was overwhelmed in the shipwreck of the year 1720 and the labors of thirty years were blasted in a single day. Of the use or abuse of the South Sea scheme, of the guilt or innocence of my grandfather and his brother directors, I am neither a competent nor a disinterested judge. Yet the equity of modern times must condemn the violent and arbitrary proceedings, which would have disgraced the cause of justice, and rendered injustice still more odious. No sooner had the nation awakened from its golden dream, than a popular and even a parliamentary clamour demanded its victims; but it was acknowledged on all sides, that the directors, however guilty, could not be touched by any known laws of the land. The intemperate notions of Lord Molesworth were not literally acted on; but a bill of pains and penalties was introduced—a retroactive statute, to punish the offences which did not exist at the time they were committed. The legislature restrained the persons of the directors, imposed an exorbitant security for their appearance, and marked their character with a previous note of ignominy. They were compelled to deliver, upon oath, the strict value of their estates, and were disabled from making any transfer or alienation of any part of their property. Against a bill of pains and penalties, it is the common right of every subject to be heard by his counsel at the bar. They prayed to be heard. Their prayers were refused, and their oppressors, who required no evidence, would listen to no defence. It had been at first proposed, that one-eighth of their respective estates should be allowed for the future support of the directors; but it was especially urged that, in the various shades of opulence and guilt, such a proportion would be too light for many, and for some might possibly be too heavy. The character and conduct of each man were separately weighed; but, instead of the calm solemnity of a judicial inquiry, the fortune and honor of thirty-three Englishmen were made the topics of hasty conversation, the sport of a lawless majority; and the basest member of the committee, by a malicious word or a silent vote, might indulge his general spleen, or personal animosity. Injury was aggravated by insult, and insult was embittered by pleasantry. Allowances of £20 or 1s. were facetiously moved. A vague report that a director had formerly been concerned in another project, by which some unknown persons had lost their money, was admitted as a proof of his actual guilt. One man was ruined because he had dropped a foolish speech, that his horses should feed upon gold; another, because he was grown so proud, that one day, at the treasury, he had refused a civil answer to persons much above him. All were condemned, absent and unheard, in arbitrary lines and forfeitures, which swept away the greatest part of their substance. Such bold oppression can scarcely be shielded by the omnipotence of parliament. My grandfather could not expect to be treated with more lenity than his companions. His Tory principles and connections rendered him obnoxious to the ruling powers. His name was reported in a suspicious secret. His well-known abilities could not plead the excuse of ignorance or error. In the first proceedings against the South Sea directors, Mr. Gibbon was one of the first taken into custody, and in the final sentence the measure of his fine proclaimed him eminently guilty. The total estimate, which he delivered on oath to the House of Commons, amounted to £106,543 5s. 6d., exclusive of antecedent settlements. Two different allowances of £15,000 and of £10,000 were moved for Mr. Gibbon; but, on the question being put, it was carried without a division for the smaller sum. On these ruins, with the skill and credit of which parliament had not been able to despoil him, my grandfather, at a mature age, erected the edifice of a new fortune. The labors of sixteen years were amply rewarded; and I have reason to believe that the second structure was not much inferior to the first."

The next consideration of the legislature, after the punishment of the directors, was to restore public credit. The scheme of Walpole had been found insufficient, and had fallen into disrepute. A computation was made of the whole capital stock of the South Sea Company at the end of the year 1720. It was found to amount to thirty-seven millions eight hundred thousand pounds, of which the stock allotted to all the proprietors only amounted to twenty-four millions five hundred thousand pounds. The remainder of thirteen millions three hundred thousand pounds belonged to the company in their corporate capacity, and was the profit they had made by the national delusion. Upwards of eight millions of this were taken from the company, and divided among the proprietors and subscribers generally, making a dividend of about £33 6s. 8d. percent. This was a great relief. It was further ordered, that such persons as had borrowed money from the South Sea Company upon stock actually transferred and pledged at the time of borrowing to or for the use of the company, should be free from all demands, upon payment of ten percent of the sums so borrowed. They had lent about eleven millions in this manner, at a time when prices were unnaturally raised; and they now received back one million one hundred thousand, when prices had sunk to their ordinary level.

But it was a long time before public credit was thoroughly restored. Enterprise, like Icarus, had soared too high, and melted the wax of her wings; like Icarus, she had fallen into a sea, and learned, while floundering in its waves, that her proper element was the solid ground. She has never since attempted so high a flight.

In times of great commercial prosperity there has been a tendency to over-speculation on several occasions since then. The success of one project generally produces others of a similar kind. Popular imitativeness will always, in a trading nation, seize hold of such successes, and drag a community too anxious for profits into an abyss from which extrication is difficult. Bubble companies, of a kind similar to those engendered by the South Sea project, lived their little day in the famous year of the panic, 1825. On that occasion, as in 1720, knavery gathered a rich harvest from cupidity, but both suffered when the day of reckoning came. The schemes of the year 1836 threatened, at one time, results as disastrous; but they were happily averted before it was too late.[4]

---

4. The South Sea project remained until 1845 the greatest example in British history of the infatuation of the people for commercial gambling.

NOTES TO CHAPTER XIII

The South Sea Bubble now appears,
Which caused some smiles, some countless tears,
And set half Europe by the ears.

(1.) Blunt, the projector, had taken the hint of his plan from the famous Mississippi scheme formed by Law, which in the preceding year had raised such a ferment in France, and entailed ruin upon many thousand families of that kingdom. In the scheme of Law there was something substantial. An exclusive trade to Louisiana promised some advantage; though the design was defeated by the frantic eagerness of the people. Law himself became the dupe of the regent, who transferred the burden of 1,500,000,000 of the king's debts to the shoulders of the subjects; while the projector was sacrificed as the scapegoat of the political iniquity. The South Sea scheme promised no commercial advantage of any consequence. It was buoyed up by nothing but the folly and rapaciousness of individuals, which became so blind and extravagant, that Blunt, with moderate talents, was able to impose upon the whole nation, and make tools of other directors.—Smollett.

(2.) All distinction of party, religion, sex, character and circumstances, were swallowed up in this universal concern, or in some such pecuniary project. Exchange Alley was filled with a strange concourse of statesmen and clergymen, churchmen and dissenters, whigs and tories, physicians, lawyers, tradesmen and even with multitudes of females. All other professions and employments were utterly neglected; and the people's attention wholly engrossed by this and other chimerical schemes, which were known by the denomination of bubbles.—*Ibid.*

(3.) Men of good estate sold house and land in order to become great shareholders; merchants of eminence neglected their established traffic to reap 50 percent of profit; and the whole nation became intoxicated with percentages, dividends and transfers. . . . Subscription succeeded subscription, each mounting above the other till the stock rose to above a thousand percent. And the insolence of the Governor and Directors rose in proportion until it was said, "We have made them kings and they deal with everybody as such."—*Civil Transactions*, 1720.

(4.) "To speak in a gaming style," said a sober financier of the day, "the South, Sea stock must be allowed the honor of being the gold table; the better sort of these bubbles, the silver tables; and the lower sort, the farthing tables for the footmen." But every day brought forth a new project till all trade was suspended save this gambling in shares—till Change Alley was crammed from morning till night with dukes, lords, country squires, parsons, dissenting ministers, brokers and jobbers, and men of every possible color and description—nay, the very ladies appeared there at times in their eagerness to transact their own business.—*Pict. History of England*.

(5.) So general had been the gambling, that one who took the pains to count the exceptions among ministers and noblemen of highest rank, could only name Lord Stanhope and the Dukes of Argyle and Roxburgh as not having been "in the stocks." Walpole, notwithstanding his denouncement of the scheme, had been deeply in it, and had been a great gainer by it, having sold out at the highest price, leaving his wife to speculate on her own account.—*Ibid.*

(6.) It was said and believed that his majesty and his ill-favored German mistresses, by buying at the lowest and selling out at the highest, had realized enormous sums, which were all carried over to Hanover, to be hoarded or spent there. It was also said that these rapacious sultanas, and some of the king's ministers as well, had received large sums in stock from Sir John Blunt, the projector, and others, to recommend the project.—*Ibid.*

(7.) The mental aberration of the public proved itself in the most preposterous demand for shares, from persons willing to stake not only every penny they had, but many pounds which they had not. The proverb that "one fool makes many," found a parallel in the fact that one knave makes many; for the South Sea schemer called into existence a number of imitators, all anxious to profit by the credulity he had excited. . . . Those who witnessed the Railway mania of 1845, can form a conception— though a very inadequate one—of the madness which prevailed in the early part of the eighteenth century under the cunning influence of Blunt, who, strange to say, was a living illustration of a marvellous misnomer, for this Blunt was the essence of sharpness, at a time when obtuseness was the characteristic of all the rest of the community. The amiable weakness which, in 1845, induced the whole population to concur in planning railways for every hole and corner of the world, the philanthropy which would have whirled the Cherokees through the air at sixty miles an hour and twenty percent profit, or brought Kamschatka, Chelsea, the Catskill mountains, Knightsbride and Niagara, all into a group, by the aid of trunklines or branches connecting the whole of them together, the mixture of benevolence and self-interest which suggested these noble achievements, cannot bear a comparison with the universality of the movement that the South Sea bubble called forth. . . . Royalty itself had not been exempt from the prevailing madness, and the Prince of Wales had been appointed governor of the Welsh Copper Company, which was to have supplied saucepans to the whole civilized world, and kept the pot boiling for the inhabitants of every corner of the globe. . . . In proportion to the extreme credulity the nation had shown, was the savage disappointment it now exhibited. The directors of the South Sea Company, who had been encouraged in their audacious swindling by the blind rapacity of their dupes—who, in their haste to devour everything they could lay hold of, swallowed every knavish story they were told—the directors, who, after all, had merely speculated on the avarice and stupidity of the rest of the world, were assailed with the utmost vindictiveness. Their conduct was brought before parliament; some of them were taken into custody, and all were called upon to explain the grounds on which these calculations of profits were made, though the stockholders were not required to state what reasons they had for believing, with their eyes shut, all the evidently fallacious promises which had been held out to them.—A'Becket.

(8.) In fact, the emanation from Law's brain caused an epidemic delirium in Europe; strangers brought their money to us, we earned ours abroad; but if all nations appeared equal in their cupidity, the difference of national character appeared after the explosion. In England, the blow was terrible, and the throne itself was shaken; members of parliament were proscribed and expelled; the rage of many terminated in suicide. In France, the luxury and pleasure created during the system, adorned its decline and survived its fall. There was a great deal of noise and very little action; embarrassment for a few, but no danger to the government.—Le Monte's *Hist. de la Régence.*

INDEX

Aislabie, John, Chancellor of the Exchequer 193, 222–223, 229–231
Alberoni, Cardinal 140
Amédée, Victor 20
Amsterdam 4, 9, 46
anti-system 40, 41, 44, 53, 54
Argyle, Duke of, 143
assignats 149–152, 158–159

Bank Act 191
Bank of England 6, 149, 150, 151, 152, 170, 191, 192, 214, 220
bank, private, *see* Mississippi System: bank, private
bank, royal, *see* Mississippi System: bank, royal
banknotes, *see* Mississippi System: bank, private: banknotes, and, bank, royal: banknotes
Bathurst, Allen, Lord 225
Begond, Madame de, 80
Begond, Mademoiselle de, 80
Belhaven, Lord 172
billets d'etat 28, 79, 124
Bloomsbury Square 12, 14
Blunt, Sir John 194, 210, 225, 226, 229, 232, 233, 239
Bourbon, Duke of, 133, 153
Braglie, Count de, 136
Bridgewater, Duke of, 198
Brignaud, Monsieur 81
Brussels 19, 133, 139, 140, 155, 227

Campbell, Captain, *see* Darien Scheme: Campbell, Captain
Campbell, Jane, *see* Law, Jane, *mother*

Canada, fur trade of 36
Cardrose, Lord 172
Carteret, Lord 142
Caswall, Sir George 231
Cesarini, Duc de, 141
Chamillart 19, 20
Chandos, Duke of, 198
Chaplin, Sir Robert 224
Chiral, Monsieur, physician 79
Colbert, Monsieur 4, 159
Columbus, Christopher 170
Company, Darien, *see* Darien Scheme: Company, Darien
Company, Dutch East India 175
Company, (East) Indian, *see* Mississippi System: Company, (East) Indian
Company, South Sea
  books of 228–229
  Chancellor of the Exchequer, resignation of 223
  Committee of Secrecy, report of 227–229, 231
  demise of 210–216
  demise of, inquiry into 219, 224, 226, 230–235
  directors
    custody, taken into 224–225
    hatred of 218–219
    prevented from leaving kingdom 220
    summoned to Parliament 224
  established 189
  first voyage of 190
  general meeting of 210–212
  Mississippi, influence of 237
  Philip V, King of Spain, tranding agreement with 190
  public credit, restoration of 235–236
  riots, caused by 213
  shares
    price, fall of 210, 215
    price, rise of 193, 197, 209–210
    speculation in 193, 195, 210, 217, 237–240
  state debt, assumption of 189, 192, 195
  trade and revenues granted 189
Company, West Indian, *see* Mississippi System: Company, West Indian
Conflans, Chevalier de, 116
Coningsby, Earl 141, 142
Considerations Upon Hard Money 11
Conti, Prince of, 47

INDEX

Council of Finance 23, 38
Cowper, Earl 142, 195
Craggs, James, the elder 229, 232
Craggs, James, the younger 211, 213, 221, 222, 229

d'Aguesseau, Monsieur 116
Dalrymple, Sir John 167
Dampier, Captain 167
d'Argenson, Monsieur 19, 38, 40, 73, 114, 115, 116
Darien Company, *see* Darien Scheme: Company, Darien
Darien Scheme
  Campbell, Captain 178–179
  colonies
    first
      demise of 175
      departure of 174
      proclamations against 175
    second
      demise of 179
      departure of 176
      doctrine of predestination, and 177
      siege of 178
      Spanish, slaughter of 178
      Tubucantee, and 178
  Company, Darien
    assets of 182
    failure, consequences of 184–185
    initial difficulties 183
    investment in 172
    opposition to 183–184
de la Chaumont, Madame 78–79
de la Motte, Monsieur 79
Demarest, Monsieur 20
Dubois, Cardinal 116, 155
Duclos, courtesan 19
duel, *see* Law, John: duel

East Indian Company, *see* Mississippi System: Company, (East) Indian
Erskine, Colonel 172
Esquiblache, Marquis de, 140
Exchange Alley 193, 195, 196, 200, 201, 209, 210, 238
Eyles, Sir Francis 224

Farmers of the Revenue 10, 26, 55, 56
Fréne 116

General Fund Act 191
Genoa 20
George I, King 141, 218, 227
Gibbon, Edward 223, 229, 233
Gleneaghs, Mr. Heldane of, 172
Grey, Lord 195

Harrison, Governor 139
Horn, Count de, 108
Hôtel de Nevers 58, 59, 60
Hôtel de Soissons 132
House of Commons 192, 194, 211, 221, 226, 231, 235
House of Lords 141, 195, 222, 226

Isthmus of Darien 167

Janssen, Sir Theodore 224, 233
joint-stock companies
  bubbles, list of 204–208
  England, speculation in shares of 197–208
  satire, and 208–209

Kendal, Duchess of, 229
King and Queen's Commissioners 12
Knight, Robert 223–225, 227–230
Knollys, Lady Catherine, *see* Law, Lady Catherine, *common-law wife*

La Rivière, Abbé 155
Lasalle, Chevalier de, 35
Lassay, Marquis of, 155
Lauriston, estate of 3, 4
Law, Jane, *mother* 3, 4
Law, John
  abilities 3, 4, 155
  Academy of Science, elected to 63
  adoration of 63, 72–73, 156
  appearance 3, 14
  birth 3
  Britain, return to after collapse of Mississippi System 141
  Catholicism, conversion to 77, 89

characteristics 3, 4, 73, 77, 82, 154–157, 159–160
Comptroller General of Finances 77, 89, 139
Considerations Upon Hard Money 11
contempt for 107, 114, 115, 130, 133, 136–137
Darien Scheme, influence upon 172
death of 153, 155
duel 4, 12–14
Duke of Orleans, influence over 77
education 3
escape from prison 4
estates, purchase of 73, 138–139
France, escape from 133
    Brussels, arrival in 139
    Venice, arrival in 140, 154
Frederick, Prince, met with 141
French nationality, assumption of 77
gambling debts 4
Indian Company, accounts with 134, 139
jealousy of 38
nervous breakdown 109
Palais Royal, fled to 130
paper money, view of 8–9
pardon, pled for 142
property sequestrated 133
Scottish economy, view of 5–6
sentenced to death 4, 14
territorial bank
    Louis XIV
        proposal to 19
        rejection of 19
    proposal, terms of 15
    Scotland
        proposal to 11
        rejection of 11
trial for murder 12–14
women, pestered by 63, 78
Law, Lady Catherine, *common-law wife* 73, 109, 155, 157
Lawrence, Mrs., *mistress* 12, 13
Law, William, *father* 3
Leblanc, Monsieur, Chief of Police 130
Londonderry, Earl of, 139
London Gazette 14
Louisiana, territory of 36, 37, 48, 237

Louis XIV 4, 19, 28, 38, 46, 78
  death of 20
  France, financial condition of during reign 29
  rejects Law's plans 19
Louis XV 39, 80

Mar, Earl of, 143
Mississippians 75, 103, 107, 129, 132, 133
Mississippi System
  abolition of 117–120, 131, 132–133
  bank, private
    banknotes
      benefits of 26–28
      duties, accepted as payment for 26
      Government use of 25
      introduction of 26
      terms of 30–31
    charter, terms of 30
    Duke of Orleans, patronized by 25
    established 25, 147
    nationalized 41, 49
    success of 26–27
  bank, royal
    banknotes
      circulation, amount and denomination, table of 120–121
      demand for 41, 73–74
      devaluation of 114
      proliferation of 61
      forced use of 92, 149
      hatred of 108
      loss of confidence in 106
      price, fixed 151
      value, decline of 91, 105, 113, 131–132, 149
      withdrawal of 131
    Director General, Law appointed 41
    established 41, 49
  Company, (East) Indian
    established 43
    income, table of 75–76
    shares
      devaluation of 114
      price, apex of 74–75, 148
      price, decline of 87–88, 91, 92, 132

    price, fixed 101, 151
    second issue, *daughters* 43–44
    speculation in 56–60, 148
    third issue, *grand-daughters* 45
    values, table of 72, 83
  Company, West Indian
    Company, China, acquisition of 42–43
    Company, East India, acquisition of 42–43
    established 36, 147
    Louisiana, territory of 38, 48–49
    renamed Indian Company 43
    trading rights, acquisition of 43
  conscription of poor and criminal 97–98
  duties, abolition of certain 69, 155
  edict of 21st of May 1720 114–115, 116, 149
    consequences of 114, 122
    opposition to, by Law 122
    revocation of 115
  jewels, wearing prohibited 91
  national debt
    conversion of 53–56
    mismanagement of 67–69
  precious metals, restrictions in use of 95–96, 113
  revenue collection
    rights of 53, 55, 69, 148
    rights of revoked 118
  riot, 17th July 1720, 130, 136
  satire, and 124, 158
  shares, market for closed 132
  South Sea Scheme inspired by 191
  specie
    concealment of 95
    devaluation of 113
    transportation prohibited 91
  speculation, effects of 69–71, 75, 92, 159
  visa 133–134, 135
Molesworth, Lord 218, 221, 233

Noailles, Duke of, 23, 38
Norris, Sir John 141, 142
North, Lord 195

Old Bailey 12

Orleans, Duchess Dowager of, 157
Orleans, Duke of,
  characteristics 23, 29–30, 38, 116
  Horn, Count de, made an example of 108
  Law, John
    influenced by 77
    introduced to 19
    view of 23
  private bank, patron of 25
  Regent of France 20
Oxford, Harley, Earl of, 189

Panama, Bay of 169
Pancalliers, Marquis de 139
paper money, *see* Mississippi System: bank, private: banknotes, and, bank, royal: banknotes
Paris, Brothers 40, 41, 47, 54, 55, 134
Paterson, William 167-172, 175, 179, 182
Philip V, King of Spain 190
Place Vendôme 83, 129, 132
Portland, Duke of, 212
Prie, Madame de, 133
Prie, Marquis de, 140

Quincampoix, Rue 46, 59, 60, 63, 69–71, 73–75, 79, 80, 82, 89, 91, 92, 103, 106, 108, 129, 139, 192

Randleston, estate of 3
Richelieu, Duc de, 157
Rochester, Bishop of, 222

Sawbridge, John 224
Solemn League and Covenant 171
South Sea Act 191, 228
South Sea Company, *see* Company, South Sea
Stair, Lord 73, 171, 173
Stanhope, Lord 222, 230, 238
Steele, Sir Richard 217
St. George, Chevalier de, 140
St. Pierre, Abbé 23
Stuart, Sir James 171, 173
Suffolk, Countess of, 143
Sunderland, Earl of, 195, 229, 232

INDEX

Tencin, Abbé de, 73, 89
Terrasson, Abbé 79
Tower of London 231
Trevor, Lord 142
Turin 20
Turner, Caswall & Co. 229, 231
Tweeddale, Marquis of, 171

Venice 20, 140, 141, 153, 154, 155
Versinobre, Monsieur 58
Villars, Marshal 83
Voltaire 40, 77, 155

Wales, Prince of, 198, 240
Walpole, Sir Robert 193, 195, 201, 214, 219, 220, 235, 239
Welsh Copper Company 240
West Indian Company, *see* Mississippi System: Company, West Indian
Wharton, Duke of, 195, 222, 226
Wightman, Captain 13
William, King 179, 184, 203
Wilson, Beau, *see* Wilson, Edward
Wilson, Edward 12, 142
Wrangle, General 139

MORE FROM NEWTON PAGE

The Life of John Law
John Philip Wood
ISBN-13: 9781934619018

John Law of Lauriston: Financier and Statesman, Founder of the Bank of France, Originator of the Mississippi Scheme
A. W. Wiston-Glynn
ISBN-13: 9781934619032

The Financier, Law: His Scheme and Times. A Graphic Description of the Origin, Maturity and Wreck of the Mississippi Scheme
André Cochut
ISBN-13: 9781934619049

Letters to John Law
Gavin John Adams
ISBN-13: 9781934619087

Newton Page books are available at all good bookstores and online book retailers. For more information about our books and how to order them, please visit our website:

www.newtonpage.com

Printed in Dunstable, United Kingdom